Portsmouth Island: A Walk in The Past

By

James E. White, III

2010

Portsmouth Island: A Walk in the Past

Published by

Mount Truxton Publishing Co.

405 W. Wilson Ck. Dr.

Trent Woods, NC 28562

Order through: info@jamesedwardwhite.com

All rights reserved. No part of this book may be reproduced or transmitted in any form or by any means, electronic or mechanical, including photocopying, recording, or by any information storage and retrieval system, without written permission from the author, except for the inclusion of brief quotations in a review.

Copyright ©2010 James E. White, III

ISBN 978-0-692-01027-3

Cover Photo: Portsmouth Village, Homecoming, 2008 by James E. White, III

Figure i. Jim White in front of Tom and Lucy Gilgo's house, Portsmouth. Photograph by Nancy White.

About the Author

Jim is the grandson of Lucy Beacham Gilgo, who came to Portsmouth Island in 1922, as the schoolteacher. There she met and married Tom Gilgo, whose family had lived on the island since the early 1800s. Jim graduated from Louisburg College with an A.A. degree, from UNC at Chapel Hill with a BA in History and Political Science, and from ECU with a Ma Ed and an Ed Spec Degree in Education Administration. He has published numerous books and articles on history and genealogy including *Home Remedies; Craven County Honor Roll, 1861*; *The Gilgoes of Portsmouth Island and related families*; *Memories of Portsmouth Island; Slavery and Portsmouth Island*; *Whichcotes of Maryland and North Carolina*, and articles for the New Bern Historical Society and the North Carolina Historical Society. He is married to the former Nancy Brinson of Reelsboro, NC and they have three sons and two grandchildren. He currently teaches history for Mount Olive College and they live in New Bern, NC.

Foreword

This project has taken many years to complete and many, many hours of work and love. It began in the summer of 1995 when I worked as a volunteer on Portsmouth Island guiding tourists through the island and telling stories of the buildings, ruins and the people who lived here. I realized then that those stories were rapidly dying out and too many people were coming over to the island and not hearing those stories. They would look at the buildings and ruins and wonder who lived there and leave not knowing the answers. Being a history teacher meant that I had to give them those answers and thus began this project.

I was fortunate enough to be raised with a grandmother and great aunt who had lived on Portsmouth and enjoyed telling me stories of their lives on the Island. I spent many hours with them and taped many of those stories. In addition, the National Park recorded many stories of the residents of Portsmouth and transcribed those tapes, making such a project easier. I obtained a copy of those transcripts and began the tedious process of plowing through them, obtaining material on each of the houses and ruins as well as the people who lived here. Then, I began digging through the Carteret County court house to get additional information to fill in the missing pieces of information. Finally, I reached out to those who were still alive and interviewed them, asking for pictures as well as specific information to make this project as complete as possible. Anyone who has additional information, photographs, genealogical information or historical information on Portsmouth Island for inclusion in the next edition of this book PLEASE send it to Jim at info@JamesEdwardWhite.com or Mount Truxton Publishing Company, 405 W. Wilson Ck. Dr., Trent Woods, NC 28562.

No project of this nature could be completed without much encouragement and assistance. I have to thank the Friends of

Portsmouth for their solid support and encouragement. They have been solid supporters of this project from the beginning and have encouraged me from day one. I have to thank Ed and Rene Burgess for their encouragement as well as their assistance in reading through the manuscript and making positive suggestions to make it better as well as writing the introduction to the book. I would like to thank Ellen Fulcher Cloud of Atlantic for her constant help, encouragement, and proofreading. No project of this nature could be possible without her help. She knows more about the history of the island than anyone and her advice and help has been most valuable. A deep appreciation goes to Chester Lynn of Ocracoke who put up with me many times and helped me as well as providing me housing and transportation over the years; to Mrs. Pearl Beauchamp of New Bern who gave me a great deal of information as well as many photos; and, especially, to Mrs. Dot Willis of Morehead City, the last living person born on Portsmouth Island, for her tremendous wealth of knowledge as well as her warm friendship. I would like to thank Karen Duggan with Cape Lookout National Seashore Park who has provided much information, criticism, as well as photographs for the book. She has been of immense help in this project. I also would like to thank David French of New Bern for his help in all the publicity for the book as well as his expert knowledge of the internet in getting my web page set up and going. I could not have done that without him. Of course this project could not have been completed without the help and support of my wife and best friend, Nancy, who shared my time on Portsmouth, who supported me those many times I went to Portsmouth without her, and all those times I spent doing research when she would have preferred we go to a movie. Finally, I want to thank my grandmother, Lucy Beacham Gilgo, the school teacher on Portsmouth Island in 1922, who taught me the love of history and the value of Portsmouth Island.

                                              James E. White, III
                                              New Bern, N. C.

Introduction

After serving nine years as volunteers for the National Park at Portsmouth Island, North Carolina, and meeting thousands of visitors, we learned of the allure this island has for a great majority of them. Many of the visitors become enthralled with the solitude, abundance of nature, and beauty of this special place on North Carolina's Outer Banks. Others come to seek information about its history and their families' connection to its past. They ask for additional background and facts which are not readily available to the casual historian. Because of this, we have become aware over the years of a need for a guide book that would provide detailed yet easy to read historical information on the peoples and structures of Portsmouth Island.

This careful and lovingly researched book, *Portsmouth Island: A Walk in the Past,* is a long time project of James E. White, III, an author and North Carolina historian. Jim's roots go deep into Portsmouth Island's past and he has delved deeply into official records, interviews with Portsmouth Island family members and other historical works to produce this book. Jim has also filled it with photographs that he uses to illustrate the stories and various family histories.

In addition to telling the story of Portsmouth Island, this book will be especially helpful for those who have family that lived here. They will be able to discover their heritage and see Portsmouth Island come alive as they explore the various structures, cemeteries, and ruins when they "Walk in the Past."

Ed and Rene Burgess
Portsmouth Volunteers

Figure ii. Portsmouth Village, photograph by J. E. White

A Brief History of Portsmouth Island

On January 7, 1971, "Seventeen men and four women braved cold wind and icy rain to attend Henry's [Pigott's] funeral in the Portsmouth Church...Henry was buried in the Portsmouth 'family cemetery,' where colored and white rest together because they lived happily together."[i] Henry's death was not just the death of a single man, but the death of a way of life—the end of an era. For with Henry's death, the last remaining two women who lived on Portsmouth Island were forced to leave their homes there and, thus, came to an end a long story that had begun as far back as 1738. Left behind were only memories, hollowed out shells and ruins that once were homes along with stories that were rich in lore and life and traditions of the sea.

In 1738, Richard Lovat received Portsmouth Island as a land grant from King George II. The following year, he deeded the island over to Thomas Nelson, who in turn deeded it over to John Kersey in 1753. In that year, the North Carolina Colonial Assembly established a town on the north end of Portsmouth Island at Ocracoke Inlet. The town of Portsmouth was to consist of fifty acres of land to be divided into third of an acre lots.[ii] The first commissioners for the town of Portsmouth were Joseph Bell, John Williams, Joseph Leech, Michael Contanoh, and John Campbell.[iii] In 1756, John Tolson purchased the first lot for twenty shillings. He was later appointed as a reader for Portsmouth by the Vestry of St. John's Parish, Beaufort.[iv]

The village grew steadily but slowly, with eight structures appearing in the village by 1770. In the 1790 Federal Census, there were "96 free white males, 92 free white females, and 38 slaves."[v] By 1860, the total population of Portsmouth, including slave and white, was over 600 people.[vi]

The soil on the island was too poor to sustain major agriculture, so the people earned their living from fishing, oystering, piloting, and lightering[1]. Most families had a small garden, a cow, perhaps a few sheep, and a horse or two.[vii]

The village continued to grow until the Civil War. In 1861, the Outer Banks of North Carolina were quickly occupied by Confederate troops who established forts up and down the banks for protection of the inland areas. By 1862, most of the same area had been taken over by Federal troops under Burnside's Expedition. As the Federal troops entered the area, large numbers of the native residents evacuated the Outer Banks and headed inland. Many of those residents, black and white, never returned after the War.[viii]

---

[1]Lightering is the process of transferring items from one ship to another in order to allow the larger ship to lighten its load thus enabling it to go over the shallow bar. Once that was accomplished, then the cargo was transferred back to the original ships.

After the Civil War, those who did return to Portsmouth, made their living primarily by fishing, oystering, and hunting wildlife. Due to the opening of Oregon Inlet and Hatteras Inlet in 1847, Portsmouth ceased to be a port of entry for North Carolina. In addition to the decline in available work, there was the danger from frequent hurricanes. The worst storm in the 19th Century was the August 16-18 storm of 1899, which is known as the San Ciriaco hurricane which completely covered the island with water, doing considerable damage. A number of families left the island following that storm.[ix] It was followed by major hurricanes in 1914, two in 1933, and again in 1944. They, along with the closing of the Coast Guard Station in 1937, and the closing of the school in 1942, signaled the death of Portsmouth. Henry Pigott's death in 1971, forced the remaining two residents of Portsmouth, Marian Gray Babb and Elma Dixon, to leave the island. In 1973-74, the State of North Carolina purchased the island and deeded it over to the Federal Government for inclusion and preservation in the Cape Lookout National Seashore.

Figure iii. Rudy Austin aboard one of his boats bringing people to Portsmouth Island photograph by J. E. White.

Portsmouth Island is located in Carteret County, just south of Ocracoke Inlet, and can be reached only by boat. The communities of people on Portsmouth Island were divided into three distinct communities: The Village, the Middle Community, and Sheep Island. The three communities were not separate islands, but were separated by creeks and/or marshes; over which bridges were placed to make travel to and from easier. The Middle Community and Sheep Island were often referred to as "Up the Banks," even though they were located south of the Village.

Rudy Austin offers boat services to and from Portsmouth Village for reasonable prices from Ocracoke Island. He can be contacted at (252) 928-4361 or (252) 928-5431. Visitors to Portsmouth Village need to carry plenty of potable water and bug spray. There is no source of potable water in the village; and at times, the insects can be rather vicious. Visitors wishing to visit Portsmouth may also do this from Atlantic, North Carolina by taking a ferry ride from Morris Marina to the southern end of Portsmouth Island. In order to reach the village from the southern end, one must travel twenty miles up the banks on the beach by a four-wheel drive vehicle. Morris Marina can be reached by phone at (252) 225-4261.

[i] Ruth Barbour, "Portsmouth Won't be the Same," *Carteret County News-Times* (18 January 1971).
[ii] James E. White, III, *The Gilgoes of Portsmouth Island and Related Families* (New Bern, N. C.: The Eastern North Carolina Genealogical Society, 1979), 2.
[iii] *Ibid.*
[iv] *Ibid.*
[v] Ross F. Holland, Jr., *A Survey History of Cape Lookout National Seashore* (Washington, D.C.: Department of the Interior, National Parks Service, Division of History, Office of Archaeology and History Preservation, 1968), 8.
[vi] Kenneth E. Burke, Jr., *The History of Portsmouth, North Carolina From Its Founding in 1753 to its Evacuation in the Face of Federal Forces in 1861* (Washington, D.C.: Insta-Print, Inc., 1976), 74.
[vii] White, 4.
[viii] *Ibid.*, 5.
[ix] *Ibid.*

Portsmouth Island

- Atlantic Ocean
- Evergreens
- Sheep Island
- Pamlico Sound
- Big Hill
- Straight Road
- Middle Community
- Village
- Beach
- Casey's Island

Part I:
Portsmouth Village

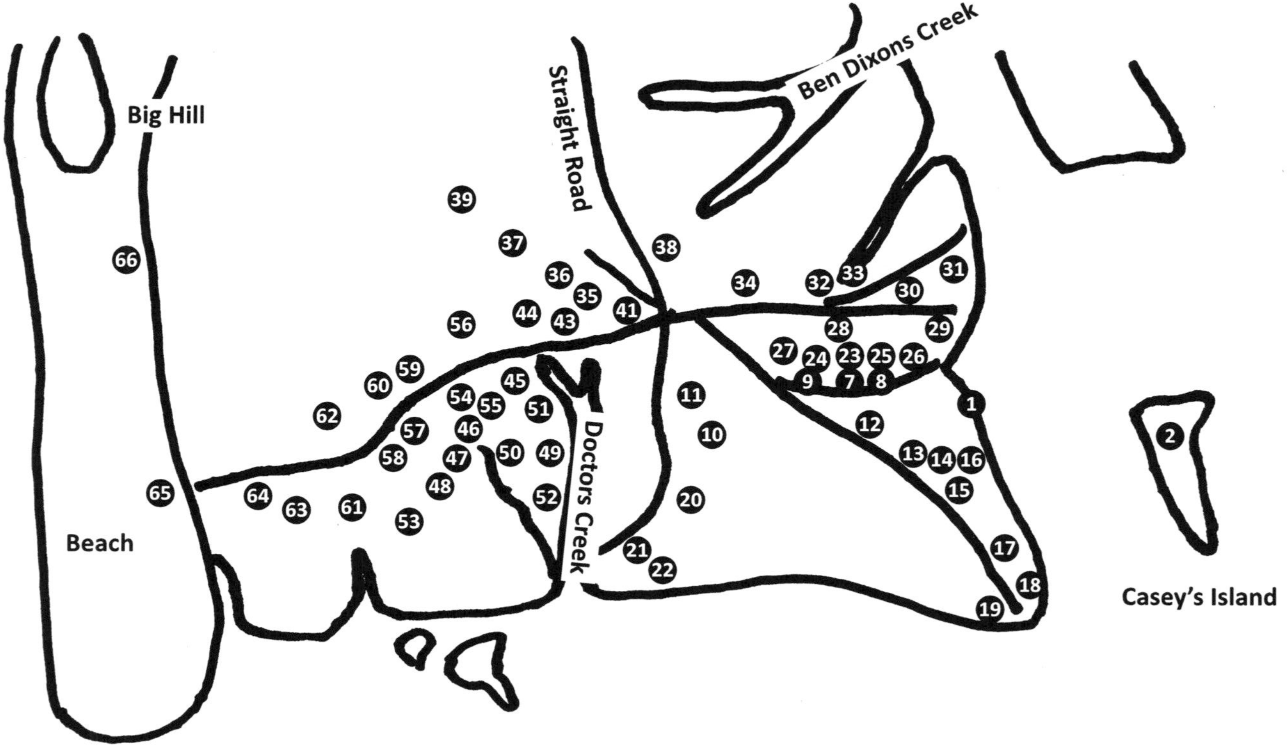

Portsmouth Village

Beach

Big Hill

Doctors Creek

Straight Road

Ben Dixons Creek

Casey's Island

Figure 1. Portsmouth Village Sign, photograph by J. E. White.

1. Haulover Dock

For most visitors, their first contact with Portsmouth Village is Haulover Dock. The name, "Haulover," originally was given to the area between Portsmouth Island and the small island seen a short distance off, Casey's Island. Casey's Island was originally a peninsula and connected to Portsmouth Island. "In the center, it was very low, and the tide would go over it. The fishermen would go and pull their boats over it…That is the reason it was named Haul Over. They were pulling their boats over that little spit of land."[1] The road from the dock into the village was built so the villagers could "drive a horse and a cart down to Haulover Point and bring up barrels of molasses, vinegar, and cider, anything that came in a barrel at that time."[2]

Figure 2. Hunting/Fishing Camp on Casey's Island, photograph by J. E. White.

2. Casey's Island

The small island (figure 2) that can be seen immediately across from the dock at Haulover is Casey's Island. Originally, it was part of a peninsula attached to Portsmouth Island by a narrow strip of land, and was about twelve times larger than it is today. It was named for Richard Casey, who purchased the island consisting of fifty acres of land on October 21, 1797, from Southy Jordan Rew for "twenty pounds current money," which he had purchased from Beverly Rew.[3]

During the War of 1812, British forces invaded Ocracoke and Portsmouth islands. It was their intent to blockade the inlet, preventing ships and boats from entering and leaving the sound. The British force consisted of some twenty vessels which attacked the American brig *Anaconda* of New York and the *Atlas* of Philadelphia. The British fleet was commanded by British Rear Admiral Sir George Cockburn. The *Anaconda* was commanded by Captain Nathaniel Shaler of New York and the *Atlas* was under command of Captain David Maffitt. Both American vessels were privateers.

In the early summer of 1813, the *Atlas* took shelter in Ocracoke Inlet where she found the 18 gun privateer *Anaconda*. Here, on 12 July, 1813, the British squadron under Cockburn, captured both vessels, taking them into the British service, the *Anaconda* as the *HMS Anaconda*, and *Atlas* as *HMS St. Lawrence*.

In the process of the British taking the inlet, the Custom's Agent at Portsmouth had been notified of their impending arrival and placed his custom bonds on board the revenue cutter under Wallace's command Captain David Wallace at daybreak headed for New Bern.[4]

The British gave chase but lost the revenue cutter and finally gave up. By that time, the rest of the British had landed on Portsmouth and Ocracoke islands, and Cockburn had given orders "that no mischief shall be done to the unoffending inhabitants, and that whatever is taken from them shall be strictly paid and accounted for." He requested that cattle be driven in for purchase and "for the Refreshment of our Troops & Ships."[5]

"The Americans claimed that the troops destroyed furniture of all kinds, ripped open feather beds, carried off clothing, and tore up the law books in the customs office. Some two hundred head of cattle, four hundred sheep, and sixteen hundred fowl were carried off." The Custom's agent, Singleton, felt that the $1,600 that was paid represented only half the value of the cattle alone. He further reported that old Richard Casey was shot in the chest, although not fatally, for being slow to return to shore when he and his family tried to escape in their boat. Cockburn was alleged to have said, "point out the man who did it and he shall be corrected," but, said Singleton, "how could you recognize one man among so many British soldiers?"[6]

Between 1866 and 1869, a menhaden fish processing plant was built and operated on Casey's Island by Excelsior Oil and Guano Company.[7] It was founded by a group of Union Soldiers who had been stationed in the area during the Civil War and had been impressed with the large number of menhaden fish in the area. They formed the company with a capital of $50,000 and built the factory on Casey's Island in 1866. The factory was supplied with modern apparatus for cooking and pressing the fish, and had experienced northern fishermen to handle the seines. However, it was found that there were much less menhaden than they had expected. The average school contained less than 25 barrels, and the largest haul of the season was only 125 barrels. It was also found that under the influence of the hot summer weather, the fish would begin to decompose in a few hours, so that the fishing was limited to 25 miles on either side of the factory. In addition, the fish taken in the sounds were found to be very poor. The average yield of oil was only 2 quarts to the barrel, and the largest never exceeded 8 quarts. At the close of the third year of operation, the business was abandoned, with a loss of the original capital and an additional $25,000.[8]

Later, Charlie Wallace and Will Webb operated a fish factory on Casey's Island, making fertilizer and saving the fish oil. Their operation cost $110,000 to build in the late 1880s.[9] The fish factory was operating as late as 1919 when George Dixon was burned to death in a fire at the plant.[10] All that remains of either plant is the old artesian well of the original factory and the foundations of the fish factory. What can be seen on the island today is a small fish camp.

Figure 3. Shell Castle from Pitcher belonging to John Gray Blount, courtesy of North Carolina Department of Archives and History, Raleigh, N. C.

3. Shell Castle Island

Off in a distance, beyond Casey's Island, one can see a small green island which is all that is left of Shell Castle Island. Originally, Shell Castle consisted of approximately fifteen acres which included a number of islands; but today, it consists of barely one quarter acre.[11] In 1789, the island was granted to John Wallace and John Gray Blount, along with other islands in the inlet. Together, John Wallace and John Gray Blount developed the island into a center of commerce and trade. They constructed "wharves, warehouses, a gristmill, store, tavern, and porpoise fishery,…as well as lightering operation" on the island.[12] (figure 3). The porpoise factory was located on Portsmouth Island. In 1800, a United States Post Office was established on the island and between 40 and 45 people were listed as living there.[13] In 1802, the second lighthouse in North Carolina was constructed on Shell Castle Island,[14] which was destroyed by lightning in 1819 and never rebuilt.[15] That lighthouse was described as "a fifty-five foot high wooden pyramid."[16] In 1810, Shell Castle Island and its buildings were valued at $130,000.[17] The island and its operations became the "key port for ocean going ships that could not pass over shallow water in the inlet when fully loaded. Large ships would anchor nearby and transfer cargo into lighter, shallow-draft vessels for transport up coastal rivers."[18] In 1810, Governor John Wallace died and was buried on Sheep Island, which is south of the village, and Shell Castle began to decline. All that is left today of the once prosperous enterprise are the brick foundations of the buildings, ballast stones, and oyster shells. In the spring, various birds build their nests and raise their young on the island where once powerful men walked; commerce was traded; and business conducted.

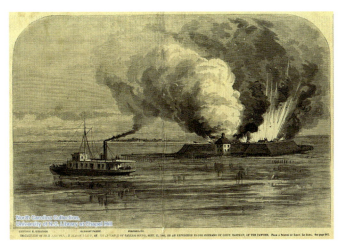

Figure 4. Bombardment of Fort Ocracoke, *The Illustrated London News*, North Carolina Collection, University Of North Carolina, Chapel Hill, N. C.

4. Beacon Island

Further in the distance and approximately 2.2 miles northeast of where you are standing, one can see another small green island, Beacon Island. "The island got its name because of two beacons that were located there which the pilots used to guide ships through Ocracoke Inlet in the eighteenth century."[19] Beacon Island was originally part of the land grant to John Wallace and John Gray Blount in 1789. In 1797, Wallace and Blount sold the island to the Federal Government with the intentions of building fortifications on the island to protect the interior.[20] By 1802, James Taylor was listed as Surveyor on Beacon Island.[21] A temporary fort was erected on Beacon Island during the War of 1812 to protect the inlet from British ships. "The cannon which were brought to the fort were... thrown upon the edge of Shell Castle Island, where they rotted and rusted. The fort was allowed to decay after the War."[22]

Fort Morgan, also known as Fort Ocracoke, was pentagonal in shape, with a bomb proof magazine in the center of the fort. It was "capable of accommodating 50 mounted guns, although no more than eight were ever installed."[23] Witterage and Wymore of Boston, leased Beacon Island in 1835 as a "place for naval stores, staves, etc. This was to facilitate the well established business of lightering."[24]

At the outbreak of the Civil War, Confederate troops occupied Fort Morgan on Beacon Island (figure 4). In September 1861, Union Forces arrived at Ocracoke Inlet with orders to destroy the fort. When they arrived at the fort, they found it already deserted. They "hoisted the American flag…and destroyed thirteen 32-pound guns along with one gun twice that size."[25]

5. Wallace Channel

Standing on the dock at Haulover Point and looking over to the right towards Ocracoke Island, one can see the channel near Portsmouth Island which was named for "Governor" John Wallace of Shell Castle. There is a dock on the north end of the island built by the National Park Service which is used by Rudy Austin to carry people over to the island and available for public use as well.

Figure 5. North West Lighthouse, photograph by Lucy Beacham Gilgo, ca. 1922.

6. Northwest Point Lighthouse

At the turn of the century, there were at least eight lighthouses of this type on the Pamlico Sound. The one at Northwest Point (figure 5) was octagonal in shape, but others were not. The lighthouse was two-stories, with a large living room downstairs with a kitchen, bedroom and plenty of closets. Upstairs, there were two bedrooms.[26] On top of the lighthouse was a big light to warn of dangerous shallow water. Charlie Keeler and his wife Annie, were keepers of the lighthouse for a number of years. (See number 33.)

Figure 6. The Dixon-Salter House, photograph by J. E. White.

7. The Dixon/Salter House

National Park Service Map # 13

Leaving the dock at Haulover Point, the first house one comes to on the right, is the Dixon/Salter House (figure 6). This house was built around 1900 in the Middle Community, approximately two miles south of its present location.[27] (See number 76.) The house was originally built by Joe Dixon,[28] who ran a general store in the Middle Community, and was a Freemason.[29] Other known Freemasons on the Islands include Wash Roberts, Dave Salter, Ed Dixon, Harry Dixon, and Earles Ireland.[30]

Theodore Salter (figure 103) bought the home and the adjacent store from Joe Dixon (figure 105) in 1929 when Theodore's wife, Annie, received the appointment as Postmistress for Portsmouth. He then moved the house from the Middle Community to its current location, taking approximately two weeks.[31] To move the house, they "used horses, which would walk 'round and 'round to turn the rope on the turnstile or spool."[32]

After moving the house, Mr. Theodore changed the roof of the house, making it a hip roof, and added on the kitchen to the rear of the house.[33] The original house had two dormer windows on the front with an A-shaped roof.[34] Theodore Salter was brother to John Wallace Salter, (See number 87), and often served as a hunting guide on the island along with Tom Bragg and Jodie Styron. "He had many wooden decoys and, like other islanders, maintained live decoys."[35] Occasionally, he and his wife Annie would board hunters in their home. "He kept the store, did commercial fishing, and worked as a hunting guide. He needed to have that many jobs in order to provide for the family."[36]

Figure 7. Mrs Annie Salter, photograph courtesy of Cape LookoutNational Seashore Park.

As for Miss Annie (figure 7), she was a "slightly built lady, with quiet reserve. Each afternoon when she came over to the post office to receive and distribute the mail, she was always freshly attired, her grey hair neatly drawn back in a bun."[37] Both Theodore and Annie Salter are buried on Cedar Island in the Community/Gilgo Cemetery there.[38]

Today, the house is utilized as a Visitor-Information Center for visitors to the Island. Here, maps and brochures of the island are available. **Open to the Public. Be sure to see the displays located inside. Public restrooms are available here. The only other public restrooms are located near the beach.**

Figure 8. Outhouse at Dixon-Salter House, photograph by J. E. White.

8. Outhouses

All homes on Portsmouth had an outhouse or necessary house as no indoor plumbing was available on Portsmouth until the 1930s. Some of the outhouses were more elaborate two-seaters (figure 8), while most were only one seater. They were also called "garden houses." The outhouse here at the Dixon-Salter House is one of the nicer and larger ones on the island. Other outhouses that remain on the island are located at the Henry Pigott House (number 21), the Elma Dixon House (number 46), the Dixon-Babb house (number 12), and the Jesse Babb house (number 54).

Figure 9. Photo of Post Office about 1953, Courtesy of Friends of Portsmouth Island, John Buckner Collection, courtesy of the History Place, Morehead City, N. C.

9. United States Post Office and Community Store

National Park Service Map # 11

According to the National Park Service, the Community Store and Post Office building was built about 1900 (figure 9) and originally was located in the Middle Community (See #76) where it was owned and operated by Joe Dixon. Around 1929, Theodore Salter purchased the store and adjacent house from Joe Dixon and moved them to their present site. There was already a store and post office located here, so he put this building right beside the one already here. The store was originally owned by Joe Dixon in the Middle Community, who later sold it to Theodore Salter.[39] He then moved it to this site along with his house. The store and post office originally had a porch across the front. The first postmaster for Portsmouth was John Rumley who was appointed in 1840, while the last postmaster for Portsmouth was Miss Dorothy M. Salter.[40]

Figure 10. Post Office and Community Store, photograph courtesy of Eula Pearl Beauchamp, New Bern, N. C.

The post office and community store (figure 10) was the center of island social life in the early part of the 20th Century. The Post Office was located in one corner of the General Store where "Pigeon holes kept mail…All the people, even from Sheep Island, got their mail at Portsmouth. "She had many open places that served as a type of mail-slot where she sorted the letters. The mail arrived by mail boat every weekday afternoon. Henry Pigott would go out and meet the mail boat. He would bring it in a mail bag from the dock to the post office in a wheelbarrow."[41] About 4:00 p.m., everyone would gather at the Post Office to get the mail. The people from Sheep Island would walk up"[42] to the village to get their mail. After the post office closed in 1959, the mail was sent over from Ocracoke by boat three times a week.

Figure 11. Interior of the Post Office-General Store, photograph by J. E. White.

In the store (figure 11), they sold "general merchandise like material, threads, and needles, supplies. Groceries included canned goods, cheese and salt pork. They did not carry any fresh meat. They did have a molasses barrel and candy."[43] In addition, they carried "gasoline, oils, and kerosene, while the others did not."[44] The store was "a gathering place in the community. Men would come and sit on the porch, whittle, and talk. They'd talk about the weather, their boats, and the best place to fish."[45] **Open to the public. See displays inside.**

Figure 12. Wallace-Grace-Styron House, photograph courtesy of Cape Lookout National Seashore Park. (Notice the kitchen on the right).

10. Wallace-Grace-Styron House

National Park Service Map # 12

The Wallace house (figure 12) was built around 1850 by Robert Wallace.[46] Later it was purchased by John Grace, who married Theresa Burgess. Theresa Burgess Grace, in turn, willed the house to Mandy Jane Dixon, who had taken care of her in her later years. She in turn, willed the house to Sarah Roberts, who was raised by Mandy Jane Dixon, after her own parents died. Sarah Roberts, daughter of Elsa Roberts, married Walker Styron, and they lived in the house in the 1920s and 1930s.[47] Walker Styron served in the Coast Guard Service here on the island in the 1920s.[48]

"The house is a 1350 sq. ft., one and one half story, wood frame dwelling on a mix of both brick and wood piers. The interior consists of six rooms, three upstairs and three downstairs, and a connecting stairwell between the two floors. Two triangle dormers are located on both the front and rear roof."[49] The house originally had a fence around it and a pony pen on the west side of the house;

the remains of which can still be seen. On the east side of the house, the remains of the kitchen and dining room can still be seen. Walker Styron bought a kitchen from a Coast Guardsman and moved it to the house.[50]

Walker and Sarah Styron lived here until they moved to Morehead City in 1944, following the 1944 hurricane.[51] Later, the house was sold to Stanley Wahab of Ocracoke and then to Jeffrey Coe before being sold to the State of North Carolina.[52]

Figure 13. Grace Cemetery, photograph by J. E. White.

11. Grace Cemetery

In front of the Wallace-Grace-Styron house is a small family cemetery (figure 13) for John and Theresa Grace and their sons. In the cemetery are buried John K. Grace, Theresa Grace, and their two sons, John B. Grace and William Grace. The cemetery is surrounded by a white picket fence as most of the cemeteries on Portsmouth were. The graves in the cemetery are as follows:

John K. Grace
Born: March 2, 1831
Died: Sept. 8, 1892
"Farewell Dear Husband
Until I Meet You In
Heaven"

Theresa Grace
Born: April 27, 1842
Died: Jan. 14, 1912
"Earth Has No
Sorrow That Heaven
Can Not Heal"

John B. Grace
Born: April 2, 1861
Died: July 3, 1883

William Grace
Born: Nov. 11, 1867
Died: Sept. 9, 1972

Figure 14. Dixon-Babb House, photograph courtesy of Friends of Portsmouth, John Buckner Collection, the History Place, Morehead City, N. C.

Figure 15. Will G. Dixon, photograph courtesy of Tommy Dixon, Oriental, N. C.

12. Dixon-Babb House

William Grace Dixon (figure 15) purchased this corner lot of the old Wallace place from Theresa Grace in 1897 and built this house (see figure 14). He was the son of George S. Dixon and Emeline Salter. George S. Dixon was a pilot on Portsmouth Island, and his wife served as a seamstress and mid-wife for the Island.[53] In 1907, William G. Dixon, who had moved to Oriental, North Carolina, sold the house to Henry Babb. Will's mother, Emeline Salter Dixon, (figure 16), moved in with her daughter Sarah James Gilgo, who was married to William Thomas Gilgo and lived in the Middle Community up the banks from the village (see #81).

Figure 16. Emeline Salter Dixon, wife of George S. Dixon.

Henry Babb (figure 17) served as Postmaster for Portsmouth from June 13, 1907 to March 1, 1919.[54] In addition to being postmaster for the village, Henry Babb also owned the community store which he had purchased from Alex Styron.[55] He also served as the Superintendent of the Sunday School at the Methodist Church.[56] Henry and his wife, Mary Dixon, had four children:

Joseph, Jesse, Henry, and Mary. Henry sold the house to Augustus Holly Byrum of Raleigh in the early 1920s. The Byrums would come to Portsmouth in the summer months to escape the hustle and bustle of Raleigh. For an excellent account of the Byrum family experience on Portsmouth, see Dorothy Byrum Bedwell's *Portsmouth, Island With a Soul*. All that is left of the original house and outbuildings is a pile of ruins, the magnificent cistern, and part of one of the outbuildings. Recently, the National Park Service has rebuilt the two-seater out house. Mrs. Mamie T. Byrum inherited the house from her husband, but due to its deteriorating state and World War II, the family no longer made their summer trips to the island. In the period, between 1970-1976, the State of North Carolina purchased the property from the Byrum family in the effort to establish the national park. The structure was in poor shape at the time of the park's purchase. All that remains of the site are parts of the brick foundation, the brick cistern and the two-seater "garden house" or privy.[57]

Figure 17. Henry Babb, photograph courtesy of Cape Lookout National Seashore Park.

Figure 18. Carl Dixon House, photograph by J. E. White.

13. Carl Dixon House
National Park Service Map # 16

This is the site of the Carl Dixon house (figure 18) which was built about 1930. His father, Alfred Dixon, owned a house on this site prior to Carl, which Carl tore down to build his own house.[58] The foundations of the earlier house can still be seen under the west end of the house.[59] Carl took over the mail boat after his father retired, and carried the mail for at least twenty years himself.[60] (figure 19). During the 1920s and 1930s, many square dances were held here. The phonograph would play and Lionel Gilgo would call the square dance sets.[61] Carl later moved to Harkers Island where he died.

Figure 19. Carl Dixon polling the mail from the Mail Boat to Portsmouth Island. ca. 1930. Photograph courtesy of Cape Lookout National Seashore Park.

14. Earles Ireland House Site

Just behind and to the west of the Carl Dixon site are the remains of an earlier house. It was the home of Earles Ireland, which was located a little to the west of the present house. Earles Ireland, the son of Daniel and Mary Ireland, was a prosperous sea captain before the Civil War, who married Matilda Roberts in 1823, daughter of John Roberts. Research shows that Earles Ireland originally owned the Sophronia Gilgo house (See number 83) but later he moved it to this site. He named his home here "The Cedars" because of the tall cedar trees surrounding it.

The house was a well built house, two stories in height, and was called a "storm house" because it had brace blocks attached to the foundation to give it added strength during a storm.[62] (For a good example of such bracing, see the Wash Roberts house, #56). The only remains of Earles Irelands' house is the cistern (figure 20) which is still being used today.

Figure 20. Cistern from the Earles Ireland house site which is located by the Carl Dixon house, photograph by J. E. White.

Earles Ireland's son, David Ireland, was a blockade runner during the Civil War and owned the Wash Roberts' house at that time. Earles Ireland also owned the grist mill located on the point. In addition, he owned a number of slaves who lived on the property, living above the kitchen in the loft.[63] Earles Ireland died in 1877 and Matilda Roberts Ireland died in 1887. Both are buried on Cedar Island. Earles Ireland's daughter, Matilda Ireland, who married Asa Mann, continued to live in the house.

After the hurricane of 1899, Asa and Matilda Ireland Mann left Portsmouth for Belhaven, North Carolina, taking their only daughter, Nina Mann, with them. Nina had taught school at Portsmouth as well as music on the island. William Grace Dixon, son of George S. Dixon and Emeline Salter, left Portsmouth at the same time, in order to marry Nina Mann.

The earliest records for this property found thus far show that the property was originally owned by David Wallace, who deeded it to James Wallace prior to 1832.[64] In 1832, James Wallace sold the property to Taylor Walker, who in turn sold it again in 1835 to Sylvester Brown for "eight hundred dollars."[65] Brown lived here until 1841 when he sold the house and property to Earles Ireland for $75.00. He sold only the house and a small lot which consisted of only two acres.[66] The Ireland family resided here until Earles Ireland's daughter sold the house to Henry Goodwin in 1901.[67] In 1904, Goodwin sold the house to Alfred Dixon for $200.00.[68]

Alfred Dixon tore down the original Ireland house and built a much smaller house on the site.[69] Alfred Dixon was a small man who moved quickly and smiled easily.[70] He carried the mail, going out twice daily into the sound to meet the mail boat and bring the mail into Portsmouth. He was paid a grand sum of $30.00 per month for carrying the mail, which he did for over thirty years.[71] After Alfred Dixon retired from the mail service, his son, Carl Dixon, took over the position.

Figure 21. Frank Gaskill House, photograph by J. E. White.

15. Frank Gaskill House

National Park Service Map #16

This house (figure 21) was owned by Frank Gaskill (figure 22) son of John W. and Elizabeth Gaskill. According to the Park Service, this house was built about 1930.[72] Frank Gaskill was a true Islander. He "was at home with the wind and the sea, and his knowledge of island life seemed limitless. He could smell out a school of mullet long before it arrived, pole a skiff through the water without making the slightest sound, steer a motor boat with his foot as he stood high to look beyond, mend fish nets like new regardless of how torn, and take winter hunters where the wild game was certain to come in. He could always eat more food at one sitting than anyone,…yet he always stayed thin and sinewy. Furthermore, he would pray the most eloquent prayers in church when asked to do so."[73] Frank never married and his house became a haven for all the stray cats on the island. He finally left Portsmouth and moved to Davis, North Carolina, where he lived with relatives until he died.[74] (See numbers 16 and 75).

Figure 22. Frank Gaskill, photograph courtesy of Cape Lookout National Seashore Park.

Figure 23. Grave of Elijah L. Gaskill, photograph by J. E. White.

16. Gaskill Cemetery

This cemetery is located about one hundred yards behind the Frank Gaskill house, headed towards Haulover Point, and can be seen from Haulover Road. There is only one tomb stone in the cemetery, that of Elijah Gaskill, (figure 23) but there are at least two other graves in the cemetery. Elijah L. Gaskill was the son of John W. and Elizabeth L. Gaskill, and brother to Frank Gaskill. The symbol on the headstone is for the Junior Order of Union of American Machinists and Mechanics. (See numbers 15 and 75).

> Elijah L. Gaskill
> Born: May 15, 1878
> Died: November 11, 1906
> "Lone is the House and sad the house
> Since thy sweet smile is gone
> But oh! A brighter home than ours
> In heaven is now thine own."

Figure 24. Tin Building, photograph by J. E. White.

Tin Building

This building has been called at various times the Fish House or the Tin Building (figure 24), either of which is appropriate. It was built by Guthrie & Jones Drug Store in Beaufort to keep decoys.[75] In addition, it has been used to store fish nets, motors, and other fishing equipment.

Figure 25. Foundation of the ruins of the Samuel Whitehurst house, photograph by J. E. White.

Samuel Whitehurst House Site

All that remains of this house site are a few bricks of the foundation (figure 25) that was the home of Samuel Whitehurst. He was the son of Richard Whitehurst, Jr. who married Sidney Wallace, daughter of David H. Wallace (born 20 May 1803). A Samuel Whitehurst married Elizabeth Parsons in 1801 in Craven County, but it is unknown if this was the same Samuel Whitehurst of Portsmouth Island. It appears that Samuel and Sidney built their house here sometime before 1810 on land probably given them by her father, David H. Wallace. No deed has been found conveying land on Portsmouth Island to Samuel Whitehurst and his father's patent was located on the mainland. Richard Whitehurst, Jr. served as sheriff of Carteret County in the early 1800s. Samuel was born around 1770. He and Sidney had at least two boys (Wallis Whitehurst and David W. Whitehurst, as well as several girls. Samuel is not listed in the 1830 census, meaning he had probably died by that date.

Wallis Whitehurst, son of Samuel and Sidney, was born about 1800 and could have been the son of Samuel and Elizabeth Parsons Whitehurst, rather than Samuel and Sidney. He married Elizabeth Wallace (born 16 March 1815), the daughter of Gov. John Wallace of Shell Castle. Based on the Census of 1840, Wallace and Elizabeth had about seven children. One of those sons was Robert H. Whitehurst, who continued to live on Portsmouth Island. More research is needed on Wallis Whitehurst.

In 1850, Robert Whitehurst gave his profession as Teacher and he was living with John Rumly. He also served as Postmaster for Portsmouth from 28 January 1850 until 18 March 1851. On 19 June 1855, he married Melvira Whitehurst, but they are not found on Portsmouth Island in the 1860 census, showing they had moved off the island.

Figure 26. Joseph Christan Jennette windmill located between Buxton and Frisco, N. C. It is similar to one that was located here. Aycock Brown Photograph Collection, Photograph courtesy of the Outer Banks History Center, Manteo, North Carolina.

19. The Grist Mill

There has been a grist mill on this site since the early part of the nineteenth century. (figure 26). A windmill provided the power to turn grinding stones that turned corn into meal and was owned by Earles Ireland and Dr. Samuel Dudley. Leah and Rose Pigott both worked at this grist mill at various times. When the wind wasn't blowing, Aunt Rose and Aunt Leah would turn it by hand, receiving 5¢ a bushel.[76] This grist mill was located on the Haulover Point near the sound where it would catch the best wind. There were two other such grist mills located on Portsmouth Island at different times.

Figure 27. Tom Gilgo House, photograph by J. E. White.

20. Tom Gilgo, Jr. House

National Park Service Map #14

This house (figure 27) originally was part of the United States Coast Guard Station complex and was built for Coast Guardsmen to live in. It was built sometime prior to 1920 and moved to this site about 1928-1930 by Tom and Lucy Gilgo. Tom paid $10.00 for the house.

The original house consisted of the two rooms in the front of the house which were used as a living room and a bedroom. After moving the house to this location, Tom built on the back section of the house which consisted of a kitchen and dining room. The house was whitewashed.

Tom Gilgo (figure 28) was the son of William Tom Gilgo and Sarah James Dixon and was raised on Portsmouth Island. His parents' house was located in the Middle Community (see numbers 81 and 82). He served in the Navy shortly after World War I. Lucy Beacham Gilgo (figure 28) was born in Beaufort, North Carolina, and came to Portsmouth in 1922 to teach school.

Figure 28. Tom Gilgo & Lucy Beacham Gilgo.

Tom laid claim to her as soon as he saw her, and after a courtship of three years, married her in 1925. After they were married, they left Portsmouth and went to Norfolk, Virginia, where he worked in the Navy Ship Yard. As the Depression grew worse, Lucy and he returned to Portsmouth about 1927 where they would at least be with their family and have food to eat. He was a commercial fisherman most of his life, although he did run and operate a small store at the intersection of the School Road and the Village Road, across from the Post Office for a brief time which he purchased from Henry Babb. They remained on the island until the September storm of 1933 when they decided it was time to leave, and moved to Oriental, North Carolina. When they left, they sold the house to Jesse B. "Jack" Bookhart and Gladus Byrum Bookhart. Jesse Bookhart was brother-in-law to Dorothy Byrum Bedwell. The back porch was turned into a bathroom and Jack and Gladus Byrum used the house as a weekend retreat. The State of North Carolina purchased the property in 1976 in their effort to establish the National Park.

Figure 29. Henry Pigott House, photograph by J. E. White.

21. Henry Pigott House

National Park Service Map #15

This house (figure 29) was built about 1900 by Harem Austin.[77] Henry's mother, Leah, got the house from Harem Austin when he left the island.[78] She had a small house near Doctor's Creek between here and the Tom Gilgo house which was nearly falling in when she moved into this house.[79] Henry Pigott (figure 30) and his sister, Lizzie, were descendants of slaves owned by Earles Ireland, who lived on the island and remained here after the Civil War. Henry's grandmother, Rose Pigott, was a "mid-wife and acted as village doctor and nurse. Rose was burned to death near here roasting oysters."[80] She and her daughter, Leah (Henry's mother), worked in the gristmill on the Island, and fished and oystered for a living.[81] Leah played the mouth harp.[82]

Henry fished for a living and in his later years, he picked up the mail from the mail boat. In addition, he clammed and oystered, and always had a garden of all kinds of vegetables.[83] Lizzie, Henry's sister, kept the cleanest house and kitchen. She cut hair for people on the Island, played the accordion and sang,[84] and had a lovely

Figure 30. Henry Pigott, photograph courtesy of Cape Lookout National Seashore Park.

flower bed around the house. In addition to Lizzie and Henry, their sister Rachel also lived here until she died in 1960. "Lizzie had a stroke and was disabled for quite a while before she died, but Henry always took care of her. They never married, they took care of each other. After Lizzie died, Henry was never the same, he was always lonesome for his sister..."[85]

When Henry became ill in 1970, his good friend Junius Austin, took him into his home on Ocracoke Island and took care of him. He remained there with the Austins until he became too ill of pneumonia. They took him to the hospital in Elizabeth City where he died on January 5, 1971, the last male resident of Portsmouth Island.

"Seventeen men and four women braved cold wind and icy rain to attend Henry's funeral in the Portsmouth Church, Thursday morning, Jan[uary] 7 [1971]. Henry was buried in the Portsmouth 'family cemetery,' where colored and white rest together because they lived happily together."[86]

The house is a two story house, surrounded by a neat picket

fence. In the rear of the house, are numerous outbuildings, summer kitchen, dairy or cool house, privy, and several water boxes. The house is painted yellow, although for much of the last years, it was painted pink because when Henry ordered the paint, he got pink paint instead of the yellow he ordered. So he painted the house with what he had.

Figure 31. Henry Pigott's Summer Kitchen, J. E. White photograph.

22. Summer Kitchens

Due to the heat in the summer, as well as the danger of fires, a large number of homes on Portsmouth had "Summer Kitchens." (Figure 31). These buildings are kitchens that were detached from the main house where cooking could be done away from the house and the fires would not heat the house nor the odors of fish and seafood cooking smell up the house. These summer kitchens originally had a fire place on which to cook, but later contained wood or kerosene stoves, sinks, and usually a small dining room. Today, the other such "Summer Kitchens " left on the island are located at the Garrish-Dixon House (number 46), one at the Carl Dixon House (number 13), and one at the Jodie Styron/Tom Bragg House (number 28), and at the LifeSaving/US Coast Guard Station (number 61). Notice the interior of Henry's kitchen (figure 32).

Figure 32. Henry Pigott and Walker Styron in Henry Pigott's Kitchen, photograph courtesy of Cape Lookhouse National Seashore Park.

Figure 33. Bragg Cemetery, photograph by J. E. White.

23. Bragg Cemetery

This small cemetery (figure 33) contains only thirteen or so graves and is named for the Bragg family buried here. Mr. Thomas Bragg was well noted for his services as a hunting guide here on the island. Rachel Pigott, sister to Henry Pigott, is also buried here. The graves located here are as follows:

Nancy Mayo
Born: Dec. 29, 1833
Died: Jan. 26, 1906
"Earth has no sorrow
Heaven can not
Heal"

James Mayo
Born: June 5, 1830
Died: April 18, 1900
"Tho lost to sight, to that
Memory dear"

Rachel Pigot
Aug. 15, 1895
March 4, 1960
"At Rest"

Georgia M. Dixon
1867-1902
"Even from
everlasting to
everlasting thou
art God"

John V. Bragg
Died: Nov. 23, 1897
Age 61 Years
"Our Father is gone
and we are left, the
loss of him to mourn.
But may we hope to
meet with him, with
Christ before God's
Throne."

Thomas Bragg
Feb. 17, 1878
March 21, 1968

In Memory of
Maria Stewart wife of
Oliver Stewart
Born: Nov. 14, 1816
Died: Sept. 1, 1894
"Blessed are the dead that
Die in the Lord"

Benjamin R. Dixon
1840-1924
"An Honest Man is the
Noblest work of God"

Jane A.
Wife of John V. Bragg
Born: June 22, 1839
Died: Jan. 4, 1899
"Dearest Mother thou hast
Left us, and thy loss we
deeply feel. But tis God
That has bereft us, He can
All our sorrow heal."

Susan J.
Wife of Thomas S. Gaskill
Born: Dec. 11, 1840
Died: Feb. 4, 1884
"Sleep Mother Sleep thy
toils Are o're. Sweet is they
rest So oft needed before.
Well have We loved, but
God loved thee more. He's
called thee our Mother to
Bright Heaven's shore"

Alexander Robinson
Born: June 5, 1843
Died: Aug. 21, 1919

Jane Ann
Wife of Alexander Robinson
Born: Dec. 24, 1864
Died: June 11, 1928
"Gone but not forgotten"

James
Son of Alexander Robinson
Born: March 24, 1889
Died: Feb. 20, 1909
"Sleep on dear James and take Thy rest, God called thee home. He thought it best."

Figure 34. Sam Tolson, photograph courtesy of Eula Pearl Williams Beauchamp, New Bern, N. C.

24. Sam Tolson's House

Sam Tolson (figure 34) was born in 1840 and was perhaps one of the most colorful people who ever lived on Portsmouth Island. His parents were Christopher Tolson and Mariah Smith.[87] In 1865, while in Elizabeth City, Sam, called "Uncle Sam" by all, was arrested by the Union army for the assassination of President Abraham Lincoln. It appears that "Uncle Sam" was "so much like the description of John Wilkes Booth, that he was mistaken for Booth. He wore the same size hat and shoes, same size in stature."[88] Members of the Wallace family had to go to Elizabeth City and verify who he was. However, some of the locals thought he was guilty and threatened "to cut his head off."[89]

Samuel Tolson married Penelope Gaskill, daughter of John and Winnie Gaskill on February 19, 1870 in Craven County.[98] Penelope or "Penelopy" died on 24 February, 1871 and is buried in Cedar Grove Cemetery, New Bern, N. C.[99] Sam never remarried and he died November 30, 1929, and was buried at Portsmouth. Recently, a tomb stone was erected in his memory by the Friends of Portsmouth in the Keeler Cemetery.

In addition to being known for his fig trees and for his arrest for the assassination of Abraham Lincoln, "Uncle Sam" Tolson was known as the best dancer in Portsmouth. "They always claimed in the old days, when he was dancing, that he carried his slippers in his pockets wherever he was so if there was a dance he could be in it. They always said he could dance with a glass of water on his head without spilling any of it."[93]

In his later years, "Uncle Sam" was a "strange looking fellow with blotched face and skin who wore a little derby hat and shuffled slowly with a cane."[90] His house stood here, near the Bragg cemetery. "He used to have a row of fig trees all the way around his house."[91] In the back of his house, "Uncle Sam" would have a small garden in which he would raise nothing but cantaloupes and watermelons.[92]

On the negative side, Sam was known as a "dope fiend."[94] "He used laudanum usually. He used Bateman drops when he couldn't get laudanum. Laudanum was his main dish but when he couldn't use that, he used Bateman drops, and he would drink paregoric if he couldn't get Bateman drops. There were many bottles around his place."[95] There are still a large amount of broken bottles located around the ruins of his house.

In the last years of his life, when he was old and feeble, Jodie Styron and Tom Bragg "looked after him. They carried him two meals a day. They didn't carry breakfast, because he wouldn't eat any. But his dinner and supper, they looked out for that man."[96] In addition to Tom and Jodi Styron helping him, the Coast Guard furnished him with wood to heat his house in the winter time. He got so feeble that he wasn't able to carry his own wood inside.[97]

Figure 35. Will Willis House. Photograph taken about 1985, photograph by J. E. White.

25. Will Willis House

Will Willis lived here (figure 35) in this small house. Originally, it was owned by his father, Jim Willis, and consisted of only one room. He always had the house painted dark red.[100] Dr. Jack Dudley describes Will Willis as a "waterman and carver, [who] guided with Tom and Jodie until the early '40s…and is remembered as being very comical and always full of humor. He was skilled with a pocket knife and carved very fine duck and goose heads, as well as some shore birds."[101] After he left Portsmouth, he opened a restaurant in Beaufort.[102]

John D. Mayo owned this property consisting of two and one-half acres of land in the first half of the 19th century.[103] Sometime prior to 1867, he sold the property to Sylvester H. Gray. In 1867, Gray sold the property to A. W. Dennis for $600.00 which still consisted of the house and two and one-half acres of land.[104] In 1896, Dennis sold the property again to Ed Keeler, who was keeper of the Southwest Point Lighthouse. Ed Keeler married Susan Dena McCotter, daughter of John T. McCotter and Narcissa E. Paul of New Bern. She was the sister of Annie Keeler who married Ed's brother, Charlie.

In 1898, the Keelers sold a small lot with right of way to F. G. Terrell,[105] the first keeper of the Life Saving Station, and the rest of the property, including the house, to James R. Willis,[106] father of Will Willis.

Behind this house another house belonging to Berry Stowe was originally located.[107] In addition, there is thought to be a small cemetery located in the area that has not been located.

Figure 36. F. G. Terrell House in Belhaven, NC. Photograph by J. E. White.

26. F. G. Terrell

F. G. Terrell was the first keeper of the Portsmouth Lifesaving/Coast Guard Station and built his house near here, purchasing this lot from Ed Keeler in 1898. Capt. Terrell was asked to resign as Keeper of the Coast Guard Station due to something that happened when the *Vera Crus* came ashore in 1903.[108] Sometime after he left the Lifesaving service, he left Portsmouth Island and moved to Belhaven, North Carolina. When he did so, he had his house (figure 36) put on a barge and floated over to Belhaven intact where it sits today as can be seen in the photograph above. It is located on main street in the 600 block today.

Figure 37. Remains of the cistern to the Williams/Daly House, photograph by J. E. White.

27. Williams/Daly House

William T. Daly (figure 38) came from Dublin, Ireland as a wireless operator. He was first stationed at Kitty Hawk, and from there, transferred to Fort Macon after the Civil War.[109] He married Claudia Williams, daughter of John and Esther Williams, of Portsmouth. This was the site (figure 37) of Claudia's parents' home and most likely, they continued to live in the same house. Later, William T. Daly was transferred to Bismark, North Dakota, where he was taken ill with typhoid fever. He was sent home, where he died shortly after arriving in Beaufort, North Carolina.[110] Claudia continued to live here with her children until she died in 1914. They are both buried here in the community cemetery.[111] There are the remains of another old house deep in the wooded area behind these ruins.

Figure 38. Capt. William T. Daly, photograph courtesy of Cape Lookout National Seashore Park.

Figure 39. Styron-Bragg House, photograph by J. E. White.

28. Jodie Styron/Tom Bragg House

National Park Service Map #18

The original house on this site was much smaller than this one and was built by Jodie Styron's parents, Elsie and Mary Styron. After they died, Jodie and Tom Bragg (see figure 39) took the house and made a camp out of it for hunting.[112]

Jodie Stryon (figure 40) married Tom's sister, Annie Bragg, and they all lived here together for fifty-seven years. About 1920, they tore down the older house or camp, and built the house now standing.113 (figure 39). Tom Bragg (figure 41) and Jodie Styron worked as guides for hunters coming to the island during the winter months. "Together they operated a gun club. Mr. Tom and Mr. Jodie were good guides. Mr. Tom was well known for his marksmanship and his imitation of the Canada wild goose."[114] They would board

Figure 40. Jodie Styron, photograph courtesy of Cape Lookout National Seashore Park.

Figure 41. Tom Bragg, photograph courtesy of Cape Lookout National Seashore Park.

them in the large house, providing room and board, plus guide service.[115] Miss Annie did the cleaning and cooking.[116] During the summer months, they would fish, but most of their income came from their boarding hunters in the winter and serving as guides.[117] Tom Bragg never married, and was somewhat of a loner.[118] In addition to serving as a hunting guide, Tom "fished, clammed, oystered, and was a market gunner."[119] When Tom was in his 80s, "he met the mailboat and carried mail for a while, relieving Henry Pigott to care for his sister, Lizzie."[120]

Figure 42. Photograph of the Abbott/Bragg House, John Buckner Collection, Courtesy of Friends of Portsmouth, The History Place, Morehead City, NC.

29. Jeremiah Abbott/Tine Bragg House

The ruins located just behind the Jodie Styron/Tom Bragg house were originally the home of John Valentine Bragg, called "Tine" Bragg (figure 42). He purchased the house from Jeremiah Abbott for two hundred dollars in 1867.[121] Abbott had previously purchased the house and ¼ acre lot from Wallis Styron in 1857.[122] It seems that Styron had purchased the house and lot from A. W. Dennis sometime prior to the 1850s.[123]

Jeremiah Abbott was born at Hammock, Maine, in 1815,[124] and moved to North Carolina about 1835, settling in Washington, N. C., where he married Mary Bateman.[125] In Washington, he ran a general store and was captain of a vessel sailing out of Washington for the West Indies until the Civil War.[126]

After the Civil War, Jeremiah Abbott was connected with the Customs service, filling the office of Deputy Collector of Customs at Portsmouth, N. C., In addition to serving in this position he also ran a general store on the island. The store was located in the area of Portsmouth called "Washington Row"[1] and was purchased from the Etheridge family in 1866.[127] Jeremiah and Mary had three

---

[1] The area known as "Washington Row" got its name from the Washington Grays who established a military fort here at the beginning of the Civil War. "When all the vessels used to come to Portsmouth, they said there used to be about five barrooms there. They could get all the whiskey they wanted and drinks."(Elma Morgan Dixon interview with Nancy Godwin, 18 August 1979).

children: Thomas, Mary L., and Emma. Mary died 2 October 1871 while still living at Portsmouth.[128]

Shortly after Mary's death in 1871, Jeremiah Abbott left Portsmouth and moved to New Bern, N. C., where he lived the rest of his life. Jeremiah Abbott died in New Bern on 18 July 1899[129] and is buried in Cedar Grove Cemetery in New Bern.[2] Also, buried in the lot are his son, Captain Thomas H. Abbott (1846-1900), Elizabeth Brent Jeremiah Abbott (1852-1910), and Maude Owen Abbott (19 May 1897 - 22 April 1978).[130]

Figure 43. John Valentine "Tine" Bragg, ca. 1866. Photograph courtesy of Cape Lookout National Seashore Park.

"Tine" Bragg (figure 43) was married to Jane Ann Gaskill and they had five children: Carolina "Lina," who married George Gilgo (see #73), Bulah who was engaged to Dave Salter, Annie who married Jodie Styron (see #28), Joseph, and John "Tom." All that remains of the original two-story house is the cistern and pile of bricks and lumber from the house.

---

[2] According to the tombstone in Cedar Grove Cemetery, New Bern, N. C., Jeremiah Abbott's death date is given as "1900." However, the New Bern Weekly Journal gives his obituary on 21 July 1899 and gives his date of death as 18 July 1899.

Figure 44. Chimney of the Ben Dixon house site, photograph by J. E. White.

30. Ben Dixon House

This house was the home (figure 44) of Benjamin R. Dixon, son of Abner Dixon and Winney Gaskill. Benjamin R. Dixon married Mary J. Davis in 1863, and remarried several times afterwards. Benjamin's children were: Ernestine, Mary, Mary F., Corbet, Adelaide, Carolet, Edith, Russell, and Estelle. Estelle was born to Benjamin and his third wife when she was age 36 and he was 68 years of age.[131]

No deeds for this property have been found prior to 1881 when Ben Dixon sold this property to George A. Griffin, Elisha C. Clark, and William C. Clark of New York for twenty-five dollars. The next year, they sold the same piece of property back to Ben Dixon for twenty-five dollars. We can only assume that Ben must have inherited the property from his father, Abner Dixon. In the 1880 census, his mother Winnie Dixon was living with Ben and they were living next to William C. Dixon, Jr. (It appears that Abner N. Dixon is the son of Sylvanius Dixon and the brother of William C. Dixon, Sr.).

Figure 45. T. T. Potter House, photograph by J. E. White.

31. T. T. Potter House

National Park Service Map #19

This is one of the oldest sites on the island, with a tavern located here in the early 1800s.[132] The earliest recorded deed for this site is 1826 when David Wallace sold the property to David Heady for one hundred dollars. The property contained 19 acres of land, more or less.[133] It appears that there was no building or house on the property at that date. David Heady in turn sold one acre of the original property to Denard Roberts in April 1840 for $20.00.[134] In 1885, Denard Roberts' widow, Mary B. Roberts, sold the property to Alexander Robinson for thirty dollars, including one acre of land.[135]

Alexander Robinson operated a store in the rear of his house. In the store, he sold brandied peaches and the men would drink liquor out of the jars.[136] He was married to Ann Dixon, sister of George Dixon.[137] Alex Robinson later sold the house to Tom T. Potter (figure 45), who used the house as a hunting club.[138]

Figure 46. Ruins of an earlier house site, photograph by J. E. White.

The original house has long disappeared, but the foundations to the chimney can be seen to the left of the house. (figure 46). The current house was built by Tom Potter about 1952.[139] More recently, the T. T. Potter house has been used by Armtex Co. as a corporate retreat.

Figure 47. Styron-Keeler Cemetery, photograph by J. E. White.

32. Styron-Keeler Cemetery

This cemetery (figure 47) is called the "Keeler Cemetery" primarily because of its location near the Charlie Keeler house which is located next to it. Originally it was known as the Styron Cemetery because the first to be buried here were the Styrons. It is also often called the "slave cemetery" because Rose Pigott, her daughter Leah, and Ike Pigott are all buried here.

While there are a number of marked and unmarked graves located in the cemetery, the most unusual one is a large brick grave which is built up and rounded over. The entire grave is covered with this brick edifice. Many people say that this grave is that of Ike Pigott, but I believe it is that of William Keeler (figure 48) because it is of the type of the late 19th century and not of the early 20th century. There is a depression just to the left of the bricked over grave which is that of Ike Pigott. This was identified as belonging to Ike Pigott by Lionel Gilgo in the early 1980s on a plat of the cemetery which is on file in the Cape Lookout National Seashore Park office.[140] Lionel stated that he had helped to bury Ike. He also thought the bricked over grave belonged to Ed Keeler, but since Ed is buried in Cedar Grove Cemetery in New Bern, NC, it cannot

Figure 48. Brick Covered Grave of William Keeler, photograph by J. E. White.

belong to him. In addition, the grave is much older than that of Ed's. Lionel knew it belonged to a Keeler, thus confirming my belief that it belongs to William Keeler, Ed and Charlie's father.

The graves located in this cemetery are:

Rose Pickett
Born: Dec. 1836
Died: Mar. 1909[3]
  "Rest, mother, rest in
quiet sleep, Wile friends
in sorrow, over thee weep"

Leah Pigott
Born:June1867
Died: March 19, 1922
"Peace, Perfect
Peace"

---

[3] Rose Pickett (Pigott), died March 2, 1909, according to Henry Pigott's Family Bible in the current possession of Rudy Austin of Ocracoke, N. C., recorded by the author.

[5] William Keeler died and was buried here on 11 January 1885. Both Charlie and Ed Keeler were originally buried in the cemetery as well, but in October 1905, their bodies were removed from Portsmouth and they were reburied at Cedar Grove Cemetery, New Bern, N. C. According to Elma Dixon, "they said that Ed Keeler was buried alive. They thought he was dead."

Isaac Pigott[4]
Born: Oct. 22, 1886
Died: July 30, 1939

Hannah Lawrence
Born: Nov. 11, 1811
Died: March 23, 1876

Ambrose J. Styron
Born: Jan. 1, 1839
Died: June 12, 1910
"Asleep in Jesus"
Dearest father we have
laid thee in the peaceful
grave's embrace
But thy memory will be
cherished till we see thy
heavenly face"

Mother
Mrs. J. D. Styron
b. Feb 21, 1851
d. April 10, 1952

Sam Tolson
Born: 11-7-1840
Died: 11-30-1929
BECAUSE OF HIS STRIKING
RESEMBLANCE TO BOOTH, WAS
ARRESTED FOR THE ASSASSINATION
OF PRESIDENT LINCOLN, BUT WAS
RELEASED UPON MANY AFFIDAVITS
    FROM FRIENDS AND LOVED ONES.

William Keeler[5]
b. 1810[141]
d. 11 Jan. 1885[142]

Eugene
Son of A. J. & J. D. Styron
Born: April 12, 1871
Died: Jan. 12, 1877
"Our darling Boy
It was hard to give thee up

Benj. G. Styron
Born: June 1, 1815
Died: Sept. 21, 1866
"Gone but not forgotten"

Figure 49. Water Cistern to the Charles B. Keeler House, photograph by J. E. White.

33. Wallis Styron-Charlie B. Keeler House

Located behind the Styron-Keeler Cemetery is an old site. (figure 49). It goes back to the early nineteenth century, but it is best known as the Keeler House because of Charlie B. Keeler, who lived here in the later quarter of the 19th century. Charlie B. Keeler was keeper of the Southwest Point Lighthouse (see #6), and his brother, Ed Keeler, was keeper of the Northwest Point Lighthouse.

The earliest record for this property thus far found is 1825, when Frances J. W. Nelson sold the property, along with 50 acres of land, to Archibald Hall for fifty dollars.[143] Four years later, Hall sold four acres out of the property to Wallis Styron for fifty dollars.[144]

Charles B. Keeler came from Wallingford, New Haven, Connecticut,[145] during the Civil War. During the War, he served as a musician in Companies F & S of the First Connecticut Regiment of Heavy Artillery where he mustered in as a private and mustered out as a 2nd Class Musician.[146]

While he was serving in the army and stationed in New Bern, he met Martha A. McCotter of New Bern, whom he married on January 29, 1865.[147] They were issued their marriage "authorization" by Jno. Walker, Provt. Marshall of the District of North Carolina and were married by H. G. Paul. Martha A. McCotter was the daughter of John T. McCotter and Narcissa E. Paul of New Bern.[148] Charles' brother, Edward L. Keeler, married Martha A. McCotter's sister, Susan Dena McCotter.[6][149]

In 1883, Charlie Keeler and his wife Martha A. purchased the property from Thomas G. Sparrow and his wife Sidney of Beaufort County.[150] The Keelers lived here from 1883 until the early 1900s, often with Charlie's brother, Ed and sister-in-law living here as well.

Charlie and Ed's father, William, came down from Connecticut and moved in with them sometime in the 1880s. William Keeler died and was buried on Portsmouth Island on 11 January 1885.[151]

On June 24, 1900, Charlie Keeler "was caught in a violent storm while returning from a trip to New Bern. He made shore at Portsmouth and was taken into the home of Mrs. Roberts who cared for him with the help of her daughter. However, in spite of their efforts, he died the next day,[June 25, 1900,] of exposure."[152] Charlie B. Keeler was buried in the Keeler Cemetery next to his father. His wife, Mrs. Annie, moved to the mainland where she continued to live until her death in 1920.

Charles' brother, Ed Keeler, died on March 20, 1905, and was buried in the Keeler Cemetery next to his father and brother. However, in October of 1905, both Charlie and Edward's bodies were exhumed and taken to Cedar Grove Cemetery in New Bern, North Carolina where they were reburied by Joe K. Willis.[153]

Charlie B. Keeler's wife, Annie McCotter Keeler died in Cove City, NC, on September 7th, 1920[154] and Edward L. Keeler's wife, Dena McCotter Keeler, died February 5, 1918.[155]

In 1907, Mrs. Martha A. Keeler, widow, of Oriental, sold the property to E. G. Dixon for $200.[156] In 1917, E. G. Dixon's son, Abner, married Mary Sneeden, the new school teacher. They lived here until the school closed in 1942, when they moved to Salter Path, North Carolina.[157]

---

[6] No marriage license has been found for Ed and Dena Keeler, but her tomb stone states that she is the "wife of Edward L. Keeler."

Figure 50. Community Cemetery, photograph by J. E. White.

34. Community Cemetery

The community cemetery (figure 50) was established in 1888 with the burial of Eugene Dixon, son of W. C. and Mary E. Dixon. The last burial in this cemetery took place in 1948 with the burial of William T. Daly, husband of Blanche Gilgo Daly, and son of William Daly and Claudia Williams Daly, whose home was located in the wooded area just to the left of the cemetery. There are approximately twenty-five graves in this, the largest cemetery on the island. A white picket fence originally surrounded this cemetery. More recently, a number of grave markers have been found in Gilgo Creek to the south of here near Sheep Island which were rescued from that creek and placed here in the cemetery.

The Graves in this cemetery are:

DIXON

Beloved Husband and Father
Harry Needam Dixon
Sept. 10, 1889
Sept. 27, 1931
"Gone Home"

Father
John B. Roberts
Born: Mar. 22, 1830
Died: Mar. 19, 1894
"No Pain, No Grief, No
Anxious Fear Can Reach
Our Loved One Sleeping
Here."

Martha
Wife of George Dixon
Born: Mar. 13, 1859
Died: Mar. 4, 1914
"Weep not my children
dear, I am not dead but
just resting here."

Wilford D. Dixon
Born: Nov. 30, 1909
Died: Nov. 23, 1922
"Asleep in Jesus
Blessed Sleep"

Lida Dixon
Sept. 19, 1888
July 26, 1961
"At Rest"

George Dixon
Born: Mar. 19, 1857
Died: Nov. 24, 1919
"Don't weep for me
dear, for my toils are
over. Someday we
will meet on The
Beautiful shore."

Mary Helen
Wife of Alfred Dixon
Born: Dec. 22, 1876
Died: Aug. 22, 1927
"Sleep Mother sleep,
Thy toils are over,
well how We love
thee, but God loved
Thee more."

George Rodnal Babb
Born: Oct. 16, 1924
Died: Oct. 18, 1924
"Our Darling Baby"

James Styron
"Our Fair Son"
James and Rebecca Styron

Caroline
Wife of William O Williams
Died: July 30, 1891

Eugene
Son of W. C. & Mary E. Dixon
Born: March 2, 1868
Died: Sept. 23, 1888
"Blessed are the pure
in heart, for they shall
see God."

Bettie Williams
July 6, 1847
Sept. 11, 1927
"Sleep dear one thy trials
are over, loved ones you'll
meet On the golden shore"

Mary H. Parsons
July 31, 1859
Died: June 8, 1934
"A Teacher Mother
and A Faithful
Friend"

Hugh Linwood Babb
Born: Aug. 19, 1912
Died: Oct. 28, 1912
"From Mothers Arms
to the arms of Jesus"

DALY

William Daly
Born in Dublin, Ireland
June 2, 1844
Died at Beaufort, N. C.
Feb. 6, 1893
Aged 49 years, 8 mos, & 4 days
"Farewell my wife and
children all, from you
a father, Christ doth call."

Masonic Emblem
Sgt. Wm. Daly Sig.Corp.
USA

Our Mother Clauda
Wife of William Daly
Born: Mar. 19, 1857
Died: Sept. 7, 1914
"Heaven now retains
our treasure
earth the lonely
casket keeps and her
Children love to
linger where their
precious Mother
sleeps."

Blanch G.
May 10, 1897
July 21, 1927

William T.
June 15, 1887
June 29, 1948

Rita Johnson Gilgo
Born: Aug. 18, 1909
Died: Oct. 15, 1911
"Rita will sleep but not
forever There will be a
glorious dawn. We shall
meet to part no never On
that Resurrection morn."

Ronald G. Willis
Born: April 25, 1904
Died: June 22, 1904
"Builded on earth to
bloom In Heaven"

GILGO

In Memory of Monroe Gilgo
Mar. 26, 1882
Jan. 20, 1927
"We loved thee well, but
Jesus loved thee best."

"Daisy"
Elizabeth Daly Gaskins
Oct. 23, 1883
Feb. 22, 1926

Elsie T. Roberts
Born: Oct. 15, 1858
Died: Sept. 10, 1914
"Thy memory shall ever be a
Guiding start to heaven"

William
Son of M. E. Roberts
Born: March 18, 1902
Died: May 13, 1902

Mary E. Roberts
Wife of Elsie T. Roberts
Born: Aug. 24, 1878
Died: Jan. 29, 1908
"A precious one from us has gone
A voice we loved is stilled
A place is vacant in our home
Which never can be filled."

Figure 51. Ambrose Styron House, photograph courtesy of Friends of Portsmouth Island, Cape Lookout National Seashore.

35. Ambrose Styron House

Going up the Straight Road, before reaching the first bridge and the Cecil Gilgo house, the Ambrose and Jennie Styron House (figure 51) was located on the left side of the road.

Figure 52. Cecil Gilgo House, photograph by J. E. White.

36. Cecil Gilgo House
National Park Service Map #21

The house (figure 52) located here was built on the site of an old Croquet Diamond by Cecil Gilgo and his wife, Leona, about 1936.[158] The land originally belonged to Billy Williams and was willed to Cecil and Leona.[159] The house originally belonged to Ben Salter and was located on Sheep Island,[160] (see number 97) but was in poor repair and nearly fell in. Cecil purchased the house from Ben for $25.00, tore it down, and rebuilt it on his location, using what lumber he could salvage from the original site.[161] "He ordered the rest of his lumber from the Moss Planing Mill in Washington, N. C. This was shipped by freight boat to Ocracoke where he picked it up in a small 16-foot skiff. This boat was small enough to pass under the bridge that was then on Doctor's Creek allowing him to off-load the lumber near where his house would stand."[162]

Cecil and Leona lived here until they moved to Davis, North Carolina, in 1942. They often returned to this site for weekend visits and vacations. Cecil died in 1995 and Leona died in 1998.

Figure 53. School House, photograph by J. E. White.

37. The School House

National Park Service Map #20

The white frame schoolhouse (figure 53) located here was the third such building on the island, following the Academy of the 1800s, and then the school located "up the banks" near the Middle Community (#78). This school building was built in the late 1920s, and housed students in grades one through eight. After the population of Sheep Island and the Middle Community decreased significantly, the building was moved to this site.[163] Students desiring education beyond eighth grade had to go to the mainland. The school is a "single story framed structure measuring approximately 36 ½ feet by 20 and ½ feet with clapboard siding and a hip roof."[164] In addition to the main building, which originally

Figure 54. Restored interior of school house, photograph by J. E. White.

contained one classroom for all grades with a vestibule, or coat closet; (figure 54) there is an eight foot diameter above ground cistern, which provided water for the school. By 1943, there were so few students left on Portsmouth, that the county closed the school, forcing the remaining residents with small children to leave the island.[165] Beneath the building can be seen the foundation of a previous building located on this site. **Please note exhibits inside.**

Figure 55. Mattie Gilgo Home, Photograph courtesy of Emma Gilgo, Atlantic, N. C.

38. Mattie Gilgo House Site

Up the Straight Road and about one hundred yards from the school house are the ruins of the Mattie Gilgo house (figure 55). The brick cistern still exists, as do a few burnt and scattered boards. Martha "Mattie" Gilgo was the daughter of William T. Daly and Claudia Williams. She married Willis Monroe Gilgo, son of William Gilgo and Emeline Robinson on July 27, 1905.[166] Monroe Gilgo joined the Life Saving Station in 1907 and continued with the Life Saving Service/Coast Guard Service until his death in 1927.[167] After they married, they purchased this house from Elijah and Lydia Dixon.[168]

The property mentions "Ballast Stone Hill"as one of the boundaries of the property. The earliest owner of this property was Archabald Hall who sold the property to Wallis Styron in 1828.[169] In 1883, the property was owned by Thomas G. Sparrow and his wife Sidney who in turn sold the property to Charlie B. Keeler.[170] Again, the deed mentions "Ballast Stone Hill" as one of the boundaries. In 1907, Charles Keeler's widow, Martha, sold the property to Elijah G. Dixon and his wife, Lydia.[171] They in turn sold it to Mattie Gilgo in 1910 for the sum of seventy-five dollars.[172]

This was a two story house with two bedrooms upstairs and four rooms downstairs, plus a kitchen and dining room.[173] Monroe Gilgo remodeled or rebuilt much of the house, adding dormers to the roof.[174] "The walls [were] ten foot high. We had a big Concord piano in there." During the 1933 hurricane, they "jacked the piano up to the top of the walls" to keep it out of the water."[175] In 1907, the schooner *John I. Snow* ran aground on Portsmouth Island. Monroe took the steam boiler from the ship and moved it to the house, utilizing it as a cistern.[176] The boiler can still be seen at the foot of the path leading towards the location of the house.

Figure 56. Mattie Gilgo, photograph courtesy of Cape Lookout National Seashore.

During the 1920s and 1930s, the Mattie Gilgo (figure 56) house became the social center of the island. "It was at the Gilgo home that preachers found welcome lodging when they came to the island. It was also there that the young people gathered several times a week for their long walks across the beach. It was there [they would] gather many evenings for typical Portsmouth parties, possibly stirring off a big batch of chocolate fudge, or congregating around the old player piano for a song fest."[177] The house burned to the ground as a result of arson during the winter of 1944-45. With it was lost most of the family pictures, Bible, and family records.[178] Mattie sold the property to Charles Henry Herring and his wife, Louise Brown Herring, for the sum of ten dollars.

39. Ballast Stone Hill

Located east of here, is the site of Ballast Stone Hill. Originally, it was named for the large number of ballast stones that covered the hill and were supposed to have been placed there as grave markers. While there is some question as to the actual location of Ballast Stone Hill, Mattie Gilgo stated that it was on her property. She also stated that Ballast Stone Hill was located near the beach and close to the Big Hill. She said that when she and her husband attempted to bury someone at the turn of the century, they were unable to do so because everywhere they dug, there was a ballast stone. She described having uncovered a grave with a woman who was dressed in red while trying to dig the grave of her relative.

Figure 57. The Straight Road, photograph by J. E. White.

40. The Straight Road

As early as 1723 there has been a road running the length of the island from the village in the north of the island, through the Middle Community, southward on to Sheep Island. This road has been called the "Straight Road" (figure 57) due to its straightness. Looking at a map of the island, one will notice very few turns in the road at all. "Stanley Woolard would dig ditches on either side of the road and use the mud to build up the road. He used only a shovel."[179] The road goes all the way to Gilgo Creek where a bridge used to cross over to Sheep Island.

Tour Directions

(You can turn back here and go back to the village or you walk on to the Middle Community. Beyond the Middle Community is Sheep Island, but you can only reach Sheep Island at this time by boat.)

Figure 58. Tom Gilgo, Jr. Store Site, photograph by J. E. White.

41. Tom Gilgo Store Site

Between the road leading to the schoolhouse and the road leading into the main village, Tom Gilgo, Jr. (see #20), had a small store (figure 58) for a while in the late 1920s or early 1930s. He ran the store only for a very short while.[180] He purchased this store from Henry Babb.

Figure 59. Doctor's Creek, photograph by J. E. White.

Doctor's Creek

This creek (figure 59) has been known as Doctor's Creek for over one hundred years. It got its name from Dr. Samuel Dudley, who came to Portsmouth in 1829, to take over and operate the naval hospital. His house and the hospital were connected together and located near the eastern side of the mouth of this creek.

Figure 60. Photo of Recently Restored George C. Dixon House after being nearly Destroyed by Hurricane Isabel, photograph by J. E. White.

43. George C. Dixon Home

National Park Service Map #10

This house (figure 60) was built about 1875[181] by George C. Dixon, son of Solomon Dixon, and his wife Patsy Williams, daughter of John and Esther Williams. He ran a general store which was located between this house and the intersection of the Straight Road, and later worked in the fish factory on Casey's Island (see #2). George Dixon suffered "spells," and one night while working as night watchman at the fish factory, he suffered a "spell," falling down and dropping his lantern. A major fire broke out, burning him badly. He was brought home where he died several days later.[182]

Figure 61. Nora Dixon, daughter of George C. Dixon, in his home, ca. 1908. Photograph courtesy of Cape Lookout National Seashore Park.

Originally, there was a summer kitchen on the rear of the house, connected with a long porch. A hurricane tore off the original kitchen, and a new and larger one with a dining room was built. This kitchen was later moved to the Garrish/Dixon house in the village (see #46).

Figure 62. Water Cistern to the George C. Dixon House
(No Longer standing) photograph by J. E. White.

44. Water Cistern

At the rear of the house, there was a large wooden cistern. (Figure 62). There was no source of fresh water on the island, so people resorted to building cisterns to collect rain water. Just before a major rain, the people would climb up on the roof of their houses and sweep off all trash and debris from the roof. The water would run into wooden gutters on the sides of the roof and into the cistern or water box. One has only to dig a foot or so on the island to find water, but the water is unfit to drink. The only other large wooden cistern left on the island is located at the schoolhouse (number 37) and at the Life Saving Station (number 61). Some of the cisterns on the island are of brick and mortar, such as those located at the Marine Hospital (number 62), the Mattie Gilgo House (number 38), Dixon/Babb's House (number 12), Carl Dixon House (number 13), Frank Gaskill House (number 15), The Life Saving Station (number 61), the Williams/Daly House (number 27), the Styron/Keeler House (number 33), and the Joe Dixon House site in the Middle Community (number 76). In some cases, wooden "Water Boxes" were used to collect water from the roof (see number 55).

Figure 63. Portsmouth Methodist Church, photograph by J. E. White.

45. Portsmouth Methodist Church

National Park Service Map #8

In 1760, St John's Parish appointed John Tolson of Portsmouth, an Anglican Lay Reader for Portsmouth Island, beginning religious services on the island. The first church building was established in 1840 when the Methodist Church was established there as the Methodist Episcopal Church, and was built on land sold by Dr. Samuel Dudley and his wife, Susan to the Methodist Church for $750.[183] The Board of Trustees for the Church were: Samuel Dudley, Wallis Whitehurst, William Dixon, Wallis Styron, and Thomas W. Styron.[184] The first church located here was a two-story structure, 36 X 30 feet.[185] It was destroyed in the hurricane of 1899.[186]

The second church was a large one with a balcony.[187] In addition, it had an organ and Bible stands. Elma Morgan Dixon remembered that it had "the prettiest lamps and chandeliers."[188] Joe Abbott, uncle to Henry Pigott, always rang the bell after church every Sunday.[189] This church was destroyed in the hurricane of 1913.[190]

The third and present church was built in 1914. (figure 63). The interior was originally varnished and kerosene lamps without mantles hung from the ceiling.[191] On the side walls were fastened copper gas lamps. They were on a swinging hanger which could be pulled out to light the lamps. "In the center were three large lamps which held about six quarts of kerosene. They had a tremendous large copper shade over them.[192] The pump organ in the church was donated by Mrs. Mattie Gilgo.[193] Regular church services were held every third Sunday, and the minister would also hold services on fifth Sundays. When services were held, they would be held on Saturday night, Sunday morning, and Sunday nights.[194] Sunday School was held every Sunday.[195] After about 1950, regular church services were discontinued. Today, Friends of Portsmouth hold regular homecoming events here at the church, and on occasion, weddings and baptisms have been conducted here.

Open to the public.

Figure 64. Garrish-Dixon House, photograph by J. E. White.

45. Garrish/Dixon House

National Park Service Map 4

The Garrish/Dixon House was built about 1910 (figure 64) and located near the Coast Guard Station,[196] behind the stables[197] and was originally built by Simon Garrish of Ocracoke. Garrish lived in the Ambrose Styron house (#35) until he finished building this house. When Garrish was transferred from Portsmouth Island Coast Guard Station, he left the house and rented it to other Coast Guardmen here on the island.[198]

About 1937 or so, Ed Dixon bought the house from Wilbert Goodwin,[199] who moved the house from the area near the Coast Guard Station to its present site. It took approximately two days to move the house to this location.[200] Ed Dixon, son of George Dixon, maried Louise Dixon. He was a Freemason and a carpenter. In addition, he earned part of his income by serving as a hunting guide with Tom Bragg and Jodie Styron.[201] The house was in need of major repairs when Ed Dixon purchased it. In addition to the repairs, Ed added the front porch.[202] The house was originally painted white, but Ed painted the house yellow.

Figure 65. Elma and Nora Dixon, ca. 1953. Photograph courtesy of Cape Lookout National Seashore Park.

In addition to the single story house, there is a summer kitchen, a cool house, a storage building, a privy, and a net house on Doctor's Creek. The summer kitchen was originally located at the George and Patsy Dixon house (#43) and was moved here by Ed Dixon,[203] for use as a wash house and storage building.[204] Summer kitchens were common place on the island, where it was a lot safer to cook in kitchens separated from the house; and in the summer months, a lot cooler. A number of buildings on the island still have their summer kitchens: the Coast Guard Station (#61), the Henry Pigott House (#21), the Bragg/Styron House (#28), and the Jesse Babb House (#54). Other items that are a part of this complex include a cool house, sometimes called a dairy or milk house. These small, open air "buildings" were built to keep milk and vegetables cool in the summer months. Chickens would often be killed late in the afternoon and hung up in the cool house until morning. A small pan of water would be placed on the floor of the cool house and the breezes blowing across it would keep the items inside cool. Nearly every house had a privy or outhouse. Some were well constructed with room for two, such as the Dixon/Salter House (#7). Most of these necessary houses or outhouses have disappeared over time. These buildings were also called "Garden Houses."

Figure 66. Dairy to the Garrish-Dixon House, photograph by J. E. White.

47. Dairy

On the Garrish-Dixon property is a small "building" known as a dairy or cool house (figure 66). This small house was used to keep milk, meats, eggs, etc. cool before refrigeration and ice boxes. They would put a small pan of water on the floor of the house and the sea breezes blowing through the screen panels would keep the items cool. There are a number of such dairies on the island. The screen would let the breezes blow through while keeping the flies out. Other house sites with a dairy are the Styron/Bragg House (number 28) and the Henry Pigott House (number 21).

Figure 67. Dixon-Babb Cemetery, photograph by J. E. White.

48. Dixon/Babb Cemetery

Located approximately fifty yards behind the Garrish/Dixon house is a cemetery, (figure 67) surrounded by a white picket fence. This is the Dixon/Babb Cemetery. There are approximately five graves in this cemetery. In addition to the people buried here, there are two parakeets which belonged to Marian Gray and Lillian Babb: Pete and Dick.[205] There are a number of depressions in the ground to the south of the cemetery, between the cemetery and the Dixon house, indicating the possibility of other graves.

Figure 68. Dixon-Babb Cemetery, photograph by J. E. White.

Those buried in the cemetery are:

Lillian M. Babb
Born: July 30, 1896
Died: January 8, 1969

Arthur Edward Dixon
Born: Jan. 14, 1888
Died: Oct. 31, 1945

Nora Elizabeth Dixon
Born: March 5, 1892
Died: Sept. 12, 1956

Elizabeth Pigott
Born: Aug. 28, 1889
Died: Sept. 12, 1960

Henry Pigott
Born: May 10, 1896
Died: Jan. 5, 1971

Figure 69. Dr. Samuel Dudley, photograph courtesy of Morgan Dickerman, Wilson, N. C.

49. Dr. Samuel Dudley House

Dr. Samuel Dudley (figure 69) was born October 27, 1789, in New Hampton, New Hampshire, the son of Hubbard Dudley.[206] He married Susan Decatur Salisbury, daughter of John Salisbury of Plymouth, North Carolina, where he went to practice medicine after graduating from Cambridge where he studied both law and medicine. They were married in March, 1828. They had eight children: John Potts Dudley (born November 24, 1829), Augustus Dudley (born March 9, 1831), Mary Catherine Dudley (born August 4, 1834), Elizabeth Dudley (born March 18, 1837), Almira Dudley (born April 13, 1843), John Wesley Dudley (born March 7, 1847), and Samuel Dudley (born November 30, 1856). John Potts, Mary Catherine, Elizabeth, and Almira died in infancy while on Portsmouth Island. Samuel Dudley, Jr. died when he was 16 in 1872.[207]

Figure 70. Dudley Family photograph, courtesy of Morgan Dickerman. (Dr. Samuel Dudley, Almira Dudley, John W. Dudley, Susan Dudley, Susan D. Dudley, Augustus Dudley.)

Dr. Dudley left Plymouth, N. C., and moved to Portsmouth Island about 1829-1830 when he received the contract as the doctor for the Marine Hospital located there. The Marine Hospital on the island was established for use by sailors in the area and the first hospital established in North Carolina. The first doctor hired for the hospital was Dr. John W. Potts, but after only one year, he sub-contracted that position out to Dr. Samuel Dudley of Plymouth, N. C. When Dr. Dudley and his wife Susan moved to Portsmouth, they purchased a two-story home, which originally consisted of two separate buildings which were actually placed together to form one house located near Doctor's Creek. All that is left of that house are the brick foundations of the original house. The original hospital had been established in Otway Burn's house and was in extremely bad shape at this time, so Dr. Dudley took two houses and put them together and used one house as the hospital and the other as his home while the new marine hospital was being built.[208]

The original hospital was "a small wooden house…which stands about two feet above the level of the ocean and not to [sic] far from its margin, upon the Portsmouth Banks and on the naked sands, without the benefit of shade. The house itself is 16 to 18 feet by 20 or 22 feet in size, without plastering or as I believe glass windows. About six cots, a pine table or two and a few benches or chairs, and the furniture of the hospital has been described. There being no cistern to contain fresh water, the water used is gotten out of a hole about a foot in depth in the sand—and such brackish and hot stuff as filters into such hole, is the hospital water."[209]

While Dr. Potts was not very successful on Portsmouth, Dr. Dudley was much more successful. "He would go to the patients, from house to house if you called him. He'd come to the patients if they were so sick that they couldn't be moved. He'd go to the home."[210] By 1850, he was one of the wealthiest men on the island.[211] In 1840, Dr. Dudley and his wife, Susan D. Dudley, sold the land to build the new Methodist Church[212] (see #45).

Figure 71. Dr. Dudley Grave Site, photograph by J. E. White.

50. Dr. Dudley Grave Site

Dr. Samuel Dudley died on May 10, 1874[213] and was buried at this site (figure 71). Sometime around 1916, his daughter, Almira Dudley Day, provided in her will that his body (along with that of his wife, Susan, and their son Samuel Dudley) was to be exhumed and reburied in Cedar Grove Cemetery in New Bern, North Carolina.[214] The original vault is still in the ground at this site.

Dr. Dudley's grave and that of his wife and son which are now in New Bern, were located here:[215]

Samuel Dudley, M. D.
Oct. 26, 1789
May 10, 1874

Susan Saulsbury Dudley
Jan. 30, 1814
Feb. 26, 1887

Samuel Dudley
Nov. 30, 1856
Sept. 9, 1872

Figure 72. Joe Abbott, photograph courtesy of Dr. Jack Dudley, Morehead City, N. C.

51. Joe Abbott House Site

This site is located approximately 40 to 50 feet behind the Methodist Church, directly across from the Sam Dudley grave site, about 10 feet into the woods. The Joe Abbott (figure 72) house originally stood at the southeast end of the runway, just southeast of the Marine Hospital Cistern. Around 1930 or so, Joe moved the house to this site due to the encroaching sand dunes, which were literally coming into the house.[216] Joe lived here (figure 73) until moving into the Wash Roberts house about 1934. Joe later moved to New Bern, North Carolina, where he lived with relatives until he died and where he is buried.[217] Lionel and Emma Gilgo lived here for a while in 1935-36.[218] Sometime later, Joe O'Neal's son took it down and moved it to Ocracoke.[219]

Joe Abbott was descended from slaves who lived on Portsmouth Island. His grandmother was "Aunt" Dorothy or Dorcas, the cook for Earles Ireland (#14).[220] She and her daughter, Rose, continued to live in the upper part of the two story kitchen behind the Ireland home after the Civil War, although most of the other blacks had left the island. According to the 1870 Federal Census, Rose had five children: Harriet, Sarah, Dorcas, Leah, and Joseph (Joe),[221] and still lived with the Ireland family. By 1880, they were still living with the Irelands, and Rose was listed separately with two of her children, Henry and Nettie.[222] Her last name was given as Ireland and the children, Dorcas and Leah, are living with Mattie Ireland (Earles' widow). They are listed as granddaughters.[223] In 1900, the Ireland family is gone and Rose is listed as Rose Pickett. Living with her are her children: Joe, Edward, and Leah, and her grandchildren: Rachel, Isaac, Elizabeth, Georgia, and Henry.[224] The Henry listed in the 1900 census is Henry Pigott who was the last male resident of the Island (#18). According to the 1900 census, Joe was born in 1870. He is listed in the 1870 census, but not in the 1880 census.[225]

Joe Abbott was the chief cook at the Lifesaving/Coast Guard Station, getting paid approximately $20.00 per month.[226] They finally went up to $30.00 per month.[227] He also cooked and kept house for Wash Roberts and his sister Jonsie, and he often helped out at the Pilentaries Club House "up the banks."[228] Joe could always be seen wearing a "white apron and chewing a snuff brush"[229] as he went about the island. He was a "soft spoken, gentle person"[230] who had little to no formal education. "He never went to school…[but]every afternoon, he would walk from his house up to [Mattie Gilgo's] home, and she would read him novels. And he'd get a hold of every one he could get a hold of he'd save and carry to [her] to read it."[231]

Figure 73. Joe Abbott House Site, photograph by J. E. White.

There was a big old pump organ at Joe's house and he would play it and sing. "He had a beautiful voice. Go by his house most anytime of night, he'd be setting there by hisself, playing that organ and singing. He sung mostly hymns—he was a very religious man and he lived his religion too.[232] In church, he sat on the back pew and served as sextant to the church. "He was always there to ring the bell on time and to light those lamps."[233]

Joe was considered to be the community doctor and midwife in the early part of the twentieth century. "When anybody was sick, they depended upon Joe to come and. . .set up with them. He gave them the medicines"[234]—herbs and that kind of thing.[235] Lionel Gilgo called Joe Abbott "The best doctor that ever lived."[236]

Figure 74. Ruins of the Net House on the Dixon Property, photograph by J. E. White.

52. The Dixon Net House

The building beside Doctor's Creek is a "Net House," built as part of the Dixon property. The net house (figure 74) is one of many such buildings built on the island to keep fish nets, duck decoys, and other fishing equipment in. Later on, boat motors and more modern equipment added their flavor to these houses. (The building no longer exists, but plans are to restore it to its original condition.)

Figure 75. Ed & Kate Styron House, photograph by J. E. White.

53. Ed & Kate Styron House

National Park Service Map #6

This house (figure 75) was built about 1933[237] by Ed Styron and originally was located on Sheep Island, approximately two miles south of here.[238] (See number 102). The hurricanes of September, 1933, blew the house off of its foundations.[239] Ed Styron then tore the house down and moved it to this spot rather than stay on Sheep Island, as no one else was on Sheep Island.[240] The National Park Service has restored this house which was in a bad state of repair. The house was affectionately called the "Kitty Cabin" after Ed's wife.[241]

Figure 76. Jesse Babb House, photograph by J. E. White.

54. Jesse Babb House

National Park Service Map #5

Jesse Babb, son of Henry Babb, built this house (figure 76). Originally, there was a white picket fence around the house.[242] After the Coast Guard Station was closed, the sole telephone on the island was located here in this house.[243]

Jesse Babb served in the Coast Guard here until 1941. After he retired, he fished, clammed, and oystered for a living.[244] Jesse could always be found playing the fiddle at the local square dances held on the island.[245]

Figure 77. Jessie Lee Babb playing the fiddle on the steps of his house, ca. 1930. Photograph courtesy of Cape Lookout National Seashore Park.

He married Lillian Dixon, sister of Ed Dixon and Harry Dixon.[246] They had three children: Edna Earl, Jesse Lee, and Marian Gray, who was one of the last permanent residents of the island.[247]

Figure 78. Water box to the Jesse Babb's House, photograph by J. E. White.

55. Water Box

Wells dug on Portsmouth Island for water would be shallow and their water would be brackish and undrinkable. Therefore, the residents had to rely on rain water to drink and cook with. One method of collecting rain water was to build a water box (figure 78). The box would collect rain water which ran off the roof of the house and store it for later use. The lid helped to keep debris out of the water as well as reducing evaporation. Nearly every house had some type of cistern or water box. Water was perhaps the most valuable commodity on the island. Other water boxes on the island are located at the Tom Gilgo, Jr. house (number 20) and at the Henry Pigott house (number 21).

Figure 79. Wash Roberts' House, photograph by J. E. White.

56. Wash Roberts House

National Park Service Map #9

According to the Cape Lookout National Seashore Park, the Wash Roberts' house (figure 79) was built about 1820[248], but it has been argued that the house was built as early as the 1790s. In either case, it is the oldest house surviving on Portsmouth Island today. The front of the house is actually in the rear where the road originally was. This house has been called a "storm house" where people would go during major storms or hurricanes. "Storm houses" were built with extra braces to the foundations to help stabilize them during a storm.[249]

During the Civil War, the house was owned by David Ireland, son of Earles Ireland, who was a blockade runner who sailed from North Carolina to the Bahamas.[250] The house was later owned by Washington Roberts (figure 80), better known as "Wash" Roberts. "There was a big fence all around Wash's house. There were cedar trees and fig trees in the yard…They had a garden to the southern end of the house and another one on the east end of the house. Wash Roberts had a stable for his horse and also a chicken coop. the stable was located in the back of the garden, south of the house."[251] Originally, the house was painted white.[252]

Figure 80. Washington Roberts, photograph courtesy of Jean Webber.

Wash Roberts (figure 80) was the Number One Man at the Lifesaving Station for many years.[253] He was a carpenter, a Freemason,[254] and "jack-of-all-trades."[255] In addition, he "made many decoys. He is remembered as jolly, good hearted, and very accommodating. He served thirty years in the U. S. Lifesaving Service and Coast Guard. Jodie Styron's mother, Jenny, was Wash's sister…He never married and moved to Oriental [N. C.] before the 1933 storm, to live with his sister, Jonsey."[256] After Wash Roberts left the island, Joe Abbott moved into the house and lived here. He had helped Wash Roberts and his sister Jonsey by cooking and cleaning the house.[257] Wash Roberts is buried in Washington, N. C.[258] After Joe Abbott left the island, Don Cheatham bought the house.[259]

Figure 81. Dave Willis/Harry Dixon House, photograph courtesy of Cape Lookout National Seashore Park.

57. Captain Dave Willis/Harry Dixon House
National Park Service Map #4

The first house remembered being on this site was a small three room house, consisting of a living room, kitchen and bedroom, all straight across and without a front porch.[260] On November 13, 1894, Dennis Mason and Joseph W. Robinson purchased "a certain piece of land on the lot of Portsmouth Township containing one acre with all improvements."[261] Dennis Mason, originally from Hunting Quarters, was living on Portsmouth as a fisherman by 1894. Dennis was one of six volunteers who went to the aid of the schooner *Richard S. Spofford* a few days after Christmas in 1894. This was the first rescue credited to the newly established Portsmouth Life Saving Station which was under the command of its new Keeper, Ferdinand G. Terrell, but did not have a crew at the time of the rescue. Dennis would be hired as a surfman in the U.S. Life Saving Service from 1895 through the spring of 1901.[262]

Surfmen were required to stay at the station while on duty and, with his family living on Cedar Island, Dennis Mason sold the property to F. G. Terrell, Keeper of the Life Saving Station on February 15, 1897 for $65.[263] Terrell in turn sold the property to Missouri Willis on September 6, 1897, for the same amount.[264] The Charles and Missouri Willis family moved to Portsmouth from Hatteras on September 15, 1896, and in the 1900 census the family members listed as living in the house were : Missouri, widow, (although Charles apparently did not die until 1921), her son, George Howard, her daughter Lena and her son-in-law, Henry Goodwin.[265] An older son, William Tice, lived next door to Missouri Willis and was a member of the Portsmouth Life Saving crew.[266]

After Missouri Willis and her family moved away from Portsmouth, her brother-in-law, Davis S. Willis, and his children began living there. Unfortunately there is no record to show if he actually purchased the property from his sister-in-law or not. The 1910 Census shows David S. Willis living in the house with his two daughters. David's wife, Emma, had died in 1895 and sometime between her death and the 1900 census, he had moved their children Sidney Farmer, Mahaley E, and Milan H. to a house near Sheep Island on Portsmouth. Again there is no deed for that piece of property. On July 15, 1905, Milan Willis married Vera Gilgo, daughter of William T. Gilgo and purchased the house belonging to George T. Parsons in the middle community where they lived until her death in 1922.[267] (see number 68).

David S. Willis, or "Dave" was the owner of a freight boat named the *Virginia Dare*. It was a vessel hailing from Beaufort, built in 1875, a schooner of 8 tons. Davie carried freight and sometimes passengers between Portsmouth and Ocracoke islands and Washington, NC. His son Milan served on board as mate and would have inherited the boat upon his father's death. Mahaley married Joseph Roberts on March 26, 1913. David died September 13, 1913, while Sydney never married and died of typhoid fever on June 14, 1918. Sometime before her death in 1918, she signed a receipt for $35.00 from Mrs. Harry Dixon for "the house".[268] (See figure 81).

By 1920 Harry Dixon (figure 82), his wife Lida, and his daughter Mildred are living in the house on Portsmouth Island and the census indicated that Harry owned the house. Even so, Milan Willis "sold" the house to Harry Dixon and his wife Lida, in June 1930 for $30.00, whose deed was recorded and gave clear title to the Dixons to the house.

Harry was a house carpenter and began to rebuild the house, fixing it as it appears today. He built the new house "right over the

Figure 82. Harry Dixon, age 18, photograph courtesy of Cape Lookout National Seashore Park.

old house and then tore the one out of the inside, and finished the inside of the one."[269] When Harry Dixon purchased the house, it was painted red or brownish in color. He painted his "new" house yellow.[270] In addition to being a house carpenter, Harry played the violin[271] and cooked for the crew at the Life Saving/Coast Guard Station.[272] Harry Dixon was also one of the Free Masons on Portsmouth Island.[273] Harry added a second story, two more bedrooms, the porches, the pillars in front as well as other touches to the house. He died on September 25, 1931, of *angina pectoris*.[274]

His wife, Lida, and daughter Mildred continued to live in the house after his death. Mildred eventually married Jake Robertson, a member of the US Coast Guard stationed at Portsmouth during WWII. After the end of World War II, he moved his family away from the island, while Lida continued to live on Portsmouth until her death on July 25, 1961.[275]

On March 30, 1962, Harry's daughter, Mildred R. Robertson, who was living in Laclede County, Missouri, sold the property to Charles D. and Jeanne B. Carrington of Roanoke, Virginia for $10.00. Later on July 28, 1966, they sold the property to Harris W. York, M. Franklin York and their wives for $1,200.00. They used the property as a summer vacation and hunting lodge until they sold the property to the State of North Carolina on January 29, 1969, for inclusion in the National Seashore.[276]

Figure 83. George R. Willis House photo taken about 1985, photograph by J. E. White.

58. George R. Willis House

This house (figure 83) was built about 1919[277] by Edward Fulcher[278] and was originally located on Sheep Island.[279] (See number 107.) George R. Willis purchased the house and moved it to this site. The house was always painted a dark red, signs of which can still be seen on some of the remaining weather boards. George R. Willis fished and oystered for a living[280] and substituted at the Life Saving Station.[281] He married Mary Elizabeth Salter, daughter of Christopher and Matilda Salter. They had two children: Clayton Willis and Mary Ella Willis.[282] After he passed away, his son Clayton Willis lived here until moving to Atlantic, NC. Clayton Willis was born 31 August 1890 and died 22 May 1988 and Mary Ella Willis was born 6 June 1885 and died 2 February 1916.

Figure 84. Roy Robinson-Lionel Gilgo House, photograph by J. E. White.

59. Roy Robinson/Lionel Gilgo House

National Park Service Map #3

This house (figure 84) was built about 1926 by Roy Robinson, Keeper of the Coast Guard Station from 1926 to 1931.[283] It was built on the foundation of the old Marine Hospital near the Coast Guard Station[284] and originally was painted gray.[285] About 1939, Lionel Gilgo (figure 85) moved the house to the present location. He and his wife, Emma, lived here until 1942, when they left the island in order for their children to attend school on the mainland. Afterwards, they used the house for weekend visits and summer vacations until his death in 1983.

Figure 85. Lionel Gilgo, Sr. Photograph courtesy of Emma Gilgo.

Figure 86. Areal Photograph of Joe Roberts House and out buildings taken ca. 1947, photograph courtesy Cape Lookout National Seashore Park

60. Joe Roberts House

The house (figure 86) originally located here was built by Joe Roberts and his wife Mahala, early in the twentieth century. He was postmaster for Portsmouth from March 1, 1919 until April 1, 1926.[286] He also ran a general store. Theodore Salter ran the store after Joe left the island, moving to Oriental. In 1926 he sold the house to E. S. Jennings of Wake County. The land was described as "one half acre where my residence is located, and including said residence, on the eastern part of Portsmouth."[287] In 1946 he and his wife Lucy Jennings sold their house and property to Harry H. Klyman of Wake County.[288] They in turn sold it to the State of North Carolina in 1976 when it became part of the National Park.

Figure 87. Portsmouth Island Life Saving Station, photograph courtesy of The History Place, Morehead City, N. C.

61. The Life Saving/Coast Guard Station

National Park Service Map #1

The Life Saving Station (figure 87) was built in 1894[289] and was one of twenty-nine such Lifesaving Stations built and operating on the coast of North Carolina.[290] Permission to use part of the old marine hospital grounds for such a lifesaving station was granted by Congress on 15 July 1893[291] with construction beginning shortly thereafter. Ferdinand G. Terrell was the first Keeper of the Station, being appointed on August 22, 1894.[292] "The station is a two-and-a-half story frame building built upon wood pilings, with a watchtower at the north end. The first floor is divided into two sections"[293] – one for the shop and the other as the keeper's quarters. "There was a fence surrounding the Coast Guard Station about 30 to 40 feet from the building except on the creek side. It stood about 4 feet high."[294]

Figure 88. Inside Life Saving Station with exhibits. Photograph by J. E. White.

The first crew began in 1897, consisting of Ferdinand G. Terrell as Keeper, with Dennis Mason, Washington Roberts, Augustus D. Mason, James T. Salter, George W. Gilgo, Jessie J. Newton, and Joseph Dixon.[295] The Life Saving Station continued until 1915 when it was merged with the Revenue Cutter Service to create the United States Coast Guard Service.[296] The Coast Guard Station continued to operate until it was deactivated in 1937. It was again manned briefly during World War II as German submarines were operating off the North Carolina coast.[297] **Open to the public. Displays inside.**

In addition to the two story station, various out buildings were located on the property. During the early 1920s, a number of small houses were built on the property to house crew members and several officers. A good example of a small house built for crew members is the Tom Gilgo house (#20) and houses built for officers include the Roy Robinson house (#59), and the Garrish/Dixon House (#46). Other surviving buildings belonging to the Life Saving complex are the Summer Kitchen just to the south of the main building, and the stables due west of the building. The stables were built prior to 1922,[298] and the summer kitchen which was built about 1908.[299]

Figure 89. Horse Stables to the Life Saving/Coast Guard Station, photograph by J. E. White.

Figure 90. Summer kitchen to the Life Saving/Coast Guard Station, photograph by J. E. White.

Figure 91. Cistern of the Marine Hospital, photograph by J. E. White.

62. Marine Hospital Site

National Park Service Map #2

There were no doctors within forty miles of Portsmouth Island in 1828, when Dr. John W. Potts came to the island as doctor of the marine hospital.[300] The marine hospital originally consisted of two, two-story houses connected together near what is now Doctor's Creek (#37), just north of the Methodist Church. The marine hospital had been established for use by sailors in the area and was the first hospital to be established in North Carolina. Doctor Potts was to receive the grand salary of $1,500 per year for his services.[301] After only a year on the island, Dr. Potts subcontracted the hospital out to Dr. Samuel Dudley, who was practicing medicine nearby at Plymouth, North Carolina.[302]

Finally, in 1842, Congress appropriated $8,500 to build a new and modern hospital facility on the island and opened it in 1847.[303] The only part of the facility left today is the brick cistern (figure 91) which was built about 1853[304] after the first wooden cistern rotted. At its height of operation, the hospital had 300 beds and 18 doctors.[305] The new marine hospital was "a very substantial two story structure, built on piers, with a fireplace in each room, primitive running water, spacious 'piazzas' and separate quarters for the hospital physician, and at times, a 'medical student.'"[306] After the Civil War, the hospital was no longer used as a hospital and was abandoned by the Federal Government in 1872.[307] Afterwards, it was put to use as a dance hall, weather station, telegraph station[308] and as an apartment house.[309] In 1894, the hospital mysteriously burned to the ground. There were difficulties with the contractors building the Lifesaving Station and meeting their opening deadlines. Rumors existed that the Lifesaving Station would open on time, even if they had to use the old Marine Hospital to do so. Just before time to open the station, the hospital burned to the ground—with no natural cause to be found.

Figure 92. Sea Captains' Graves, photograph by J. E. White.

63. The Sea Captains' Graves

Located northeast of the Coast Guard Station, these graves (figure 92) are located in an area that was quite developed in the early half of the 19th century. Numerous houses and several cemeteries were located around this site.

The two sea captains buried here were washed up on the beach at Portsmouth and their families provided their tombstones. Capt. Thomas W. Green was frozen solid when his body washed ashore in January, 1810. The other captain was Capt. William Hilzey, a black seaman, whose body washed ashore in October, 1821.[310]

> The two tombstones are:
> "To the Memory of Capt. Thomas W. Greene
> Of Providence, R. I. Who died January 17, 1810
> In the 32nd Year of his age"
>
> "In Memory of Capt. William Hilzey
> Who
> Died October 4, 1821
> Aged 36 years, 2 months, 27 days"

Figure 93. National Park Public Toilets, photograph by J. E. White.

64. National Park Public Toilets

Located on the way to the beach are public toilets (figure 93). They are compost toilets available for both male and female. The only other public toilet facility on the island is at the Welcome Center near Haulover Dock where you arrived.

Figure 94. Mud Flats, photograph by J. E. White.

65. Mud Flats

Located approximately a quarter of a mile to the east of the sea captains' graves, is the beach and the Atlantic Ocean. To the north of the graves, is Wallace Channel. There is a small dock located there built by the National Park Service. South of this direction, approximately 18 miles, is Morris Ferry and Kabins. The ferry runs from the southern end of the island to Atlantic and back, carrying passengers and vehicles.

The mud flats (figure 94) between the shrub area and the ocean and beach flood regularly, especially when the wind is from the northeast. The water will often reach a depth of six to eight inches between here and the sand dunes on the opposite side. All along the beach, various birds make their nests during the summer, as well as turtles which come inland to lay their eggs. These areas are marked as restricted to protect the nests of the various wildlife which inhabit the area. In the ocean, dolphins can often be seen playing in the distance, and on occasion, a whale may be seen.

66. Charles Wallace Cemetery

Located on the beach, approximately one mile south of here, was the Charles Wallace Cemetery. He built his house about 1850 on the western end of the island. (see #10). The only grave remembered in that cemetery was that of Elizabeth Wallace. This grave is no longer visible and has not been located or seen in the last thirty or forty years. However, many older residents of the island remember the grave.[311]

Figure 95. Thomas Truxton

Mount Truxton

On the 1806 map of Portsmouth Island, there is clearly written, "Mount Truxton." Many people have made the attempt to discover what that refers to, to no avail. While this article might not solve that mystery completely, perhaps it will shed some light on the subject which will enable some future historian to solve the mystery of "Mount Truxton."

It is quite sure that Mount Truxton has something to do with Commodore Thomas Truxton (figure 95) who distinguished himself as a privateer during the American Revolution and later as the premiere U. S. Naval captain during the Quasi-War with France between 1794 and 1801. Between the Revolution and his term in the U. S. Navy, he served eight years as a merchantman traveling up and down the east coast of the United States. He served as captain of the *USS Independence* and later as captain of the *USS Constellation*. His name was famous up and down the east coast as the most famous Naval Officer after John Paul Jones. During the American Revolution, his ship, the *USS Independence*, while attempting to enter Ocracoke Inlet, went aground on Portsmouth Island. The ship was commanded by Capt. John Robertson at that time and there is no evidence that Capt. Truxton was aboard the ship. The ship was wrecked on April 24, 1778 and contained dispatches from France to the American colonies.

Perhaps the shipwreck was used to build a house on Portsmouth Island and that house was thus called "Mount Truxton." Or perhaps, the wreck created a sand dune on the island and that sand dune became "Mount Truxton." Thomas Truxton did not purchase land on Portsmouth Island as far as can be found. Could it be that the "Big Hill" on Portsmouth Island was built upon the wreck of Truxton's ship and thus originally called, Mount Truxton? At this point in time, one can only speculate, but to be sure, it is connected with Commodore Thomas Truxton in some mysterious way.

Tour Directions

Note: This ends the tour of Portsmouth Village. You may now return to the Visitor Center or you may return to the Straight Road and take the tour of the Middle Community.

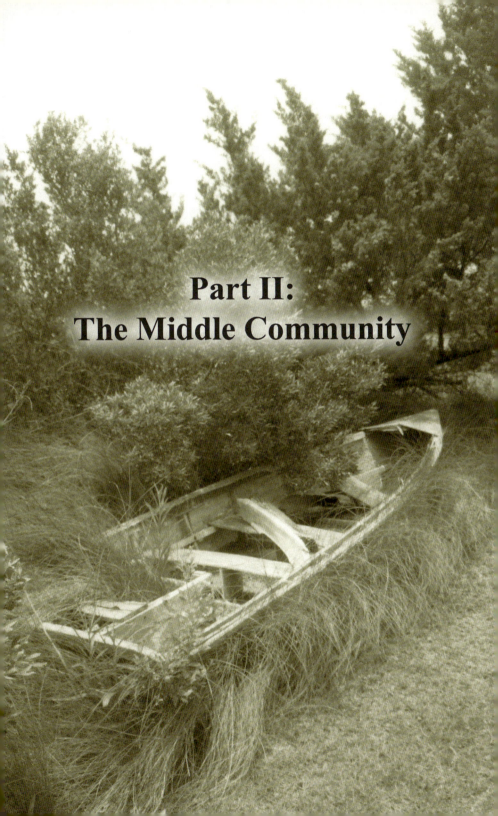

Part II:
The Middle Community

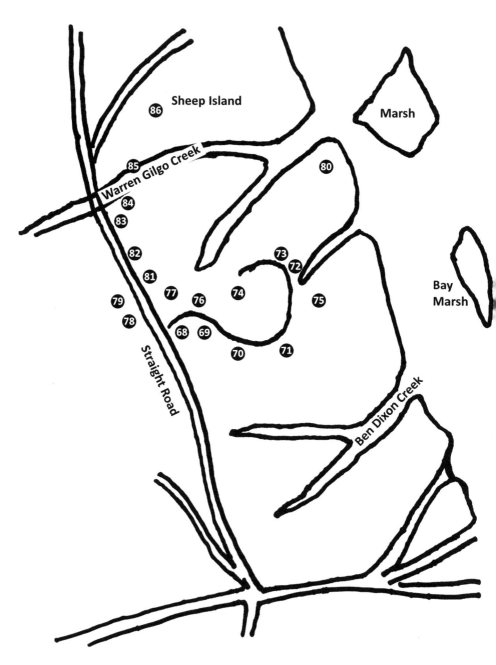

The Middle Community

67. The Middle Community

The communities of people on Portsmouth Island were divided into three distinct communities: The Village, the Middle Community, and Sheep Island. The three communities were not separate islands, but were separated by creeks and/or marshes; over which bridges were placed to make travel to and from easier. The Middle Community and Sheep Island were often referred to as "Up the Banks," even though they were located south of the Village.

Today, very little evidence of the former life in these areas can be found. The Middle Community was nearly completely burned out in the early 1960s by a wild fire that swept through the area, burning all the homes that remained. A search through the area today turns up only a few burnt pilings or a tumbled down chimney or two, but little else. Rose bushes bloom in the summertime where children used to play.

In the Middle Community were located the Old Academy, the school house in use prior to the current building further north (#37), and the Primitive Baptist Church. Several cemeteries were located here including the Gilgo family cemetery which today is under water in Warren Gilgo Creek. Joe Dixon lived here and operated a general store, as did Tom Gilgo, Jr. Theodore Salter's house was originally located here prior to his moving it to the village. Milan Willis, Zach Salter, Jim Parson, George Gilgo, Warren Gilgo, Bill Gilgo, Steve Gaskill, and Jim Roberts all lived, worked, and raised their children here in the Middle Community, and the ruins of their houses can be found there today.

68. Milan Willis House

The Straight Road forks. Take the right or west fork of the road which leads to the Middle Community and the left fork or south fork leads on towards Sheep Island. The first house site on the right side of the fork in the road going into the Middle Community is the Milan Willis house. Milan Willis, (figure 96) son of David Willis, married Vera Gilgo, daughter of William Gilgo and Emeline Robinson. Milan often served as a hunting guide[312] on the island and ran a fish house.[313] He also owned a skiff named *The Virginia Dare*.[314] In the early 1900s, Vera played the organ for the

Figure 96 Milan Willis and his daughter, Lida Mae Willis.

Methodist Church and directed church plays and music recitals on Portsmouth. In addition, she served as treasurer and superintendent of the Sunday School. She died in 1922 and is buried in the Middle Community behind George Gilgo's house, near the sound. After her death, Milan moved to Atlantic where he lived until his death in 1966. They had two children: a son Myron who died only a few days old in 1907, and a daughter, Lieda Mae.[315] Their home was one of those burned in the 1960 fire.

69. Zach Salter House

This is the site of the Zachariah (Zach) Salter home place. He was the son of Christopher Thomas Salter and Matilda Styron,[316] and brother to John Wallace Salter (See number 74). Zach was born 22 March 1859 and was married three times: 1. Rebecca English, 2. Annie Robinson, and 3. Mozell Meekins.[317] He died 27 April 1917.

Zach Salter fished for a living and had a fair complexion and red hair.[318] Zach Salter died in 1917 and is buried in the Lola Cemetery with his sister, Mary, and his parents Christopher Salter and Matilda Styron Salter. After Zach and Annie died, Matilda was raised by James W. Gilgo.

Zach Salter and Rebecca English (22 January 1857 - 15 November 1895) had seven children: Christopher Thomas (drowned when he was 17), Samuel, Malcolm, James (died at birth), Eva, Major, and Matilda Salter.

By his second wife, Zilphia Anne Robinson (Annie) (1863 - 24 December 1902), he had one child: Bessie. By his third wife, Mozell Meekins (5 December 1877 - 6 November 1938), he had one child: Hulda E. Salter. After Zach Salter died in 1917, his third wife Mozell remarried to Stanley O'Neal of Ocracoke.

Figure 97. James Parsons (1852-1911).
Photograph from *Craven County Heritage Book*.

70. Jim Parsons House Site

In the 1850 Federal Census, there is a Joseph Oliver Parsons listed along with his wife Amelia Simpson and their children Joseph, Samuel, and George.[319] In 1860, Joseph had disappeared, but his family still resided at Portsmouth, plus an additional son, James Parsons. In addition to the Joseph Parsons' family, there was a second Parsons' family residing on Portsmouth, that of James Parsons (figure 97). James was listed as a fisherman and lived with his wife Mary and their three children: Malinda, James, and May in the Middle Community near Zach Styron.[320] No relationship between this James Parsons and the Joseph Parsons' family has been established. James Parsons was most probably Joseph's (~1825 - >1880) brother and also Thomas' (~1830 - >1880) brother. See 1870 Craven County Census. Craven County Marriage Bonds, Vol. 2, 15 February 1843.

The Joseph Parsons' family moved to New Bern, North Carolina, during the Civil War, where they remained.[321] As for the James Parsons' family, they cannot be found in the 1870 or 1880 Federal Census for Portsmouth. They do reappear in the 1900 Federal Census, still living in the Middle Community. Only now, the Parsons we have living there, is James, the son of the James listed in the 1860 census.[322] This James is listed as a fisherman as was his father before him. He married Helen A. Dixon,[323] and they had three children: Alice, James, and Frederic.[324] By the 1910 Census, they had disappeared again.

Buried at Ocracoke, North Carolina, are James E. Parsons, son of James Parsons and Helen Dixon, and James E. Parsons' two children who died in infancy: George Lewis Parsons and Mary Susan Parsons.[325] James E. Parsons married Mary Eliza Jackson[326] and his tombstone records that he was born in 1891 at New Bern, North Carolina. He was 48 years old, and must have moved to Ocracoke early in the 1900s, where he lived until his death in 1939. Jim and Mary Eliza Parsons had thirteen children.

Figure 98. Lemmie Gilgo during World War I,
photograph courtesy of Virginia Allen, New Bern, N. C.

71. Lemmie Gilgo

This was the original home site of Lemmie Gilgo (figure 98), first child of William Thomas Gilgo and Sarah James Dixon who was born 25 November 1895 on Portsmouth. He served during World War I where he was wounded during a German gas attack. After the war, he married Louisa Spencer, daughter of Edward D. Spencer and Sarah Jane Gaskins of Ocracoke. They lived here until his father moved to the Jim Roberts' House. Then Lemmie and Louisa moved into the original Tom Gilgo, Sr. house (see number 82) where they remained until they left Portsmouth in 1933 when they moved to Oriental, N. C. Louisa died 14 February 1937 and is buried at Ocracoke, N. C. Lemmie died 16 August 1972, and is buried at the National Cemetery in New Bern, N. C. Lemmie and Louisa had four children: Sarah, Virginia, Ronald Linwood, and Mary Roseland Gilgo.

Figure 99. Vera Willis Cemetery, photograph courtesy of Michael Rikard, Cape Lookout National Sea Shore Park.

72. Vera Gilgo Willis Cemetery

Located at George Gilgo's house site and near the sound, is the Vera Gilgo Willis Cemetery (figure 99). Vera Gilgo, daughter of William Thomas Gilgo and Emeline Robinson Gilgo, was George Gilgo's sister and she married Milan Willis. She and her son are both buried here in this small cemetery.

Figure 100. Vera Willis Grave, photograph courtesy of Michael Rikard, Cape Lookout National Sea Shore Park.

Vera
Wife of M. H. Willis
Born: Oct. 19, 1886
Died: Oct. 5, 1922
Blessed are the dead,
That died in the Name of the Lord

Figure 101. Myron Willis Grave, photograph courtesy of Michael Rikard, Cape Lookout National Sea Shore Park.

Myron M. Willis
Born: July 7, 1907
Died: July 21, 1907
Safe in the Arms of Jesus

Figure 102. George and Lina Gilgo, photograph courtesy of Cape Lookout National Seashore Park.

73. George Gilgo House Site

The George Gilgo home site is located in the first hammock beyond the marshes towards the west, within the Middle Community. George Wallis Gilgo (figure 102) was the second child of William Gilgo and Emeline Robinson. He served as a crew member of the Lifesaving Station on Portsmouth and a member of the Primitive Baptist Church. He married Carolina "Lina" Bragg, daughter of John Valentine Bragg and Jane Ann Bragg (see number 29). He made his living primarily as a commercial fisherman and Lina taught school on the island. In addition, George served as a hunting guide on the island and was well known for his expertise hunting geese. In 1950, Lina became ill and they moved to Atlantic to live with Milan Willis. She died later that year, and he died in 1957. Both are buried at Cedar Island in the Community Cemetery.

Today, all that can be found of the original house is the foundation to the chimney, the fence posts of a pen for the animals, and remnants of her roses blooming all around the site.

125

Figure 103. Theodore Salter, photograph courtesy of Pearl Beauchamp, New Bern, N. C.

74. Theodore Salter Home Site

Theodore Salter (figure 103) originally lived at this site, before purchasing the Joe Dixon house and store, and moving them to the Village. He sold this house to George Brooks who lived here afterwards. The most striking feature of this site is the tremendous oak tree. The original house burned in the fire about 1960.[327] (For more on Theodore Salter, see number 7).

75. Steve Gaskill House Site

Located about 150 to 200 yards north and west of the Lemmie Gilgo house site, are the remains of the Stephen A. Gaskill house.[328] At this point, the area is so grown up with underbrush, trees and vines that these ruins have not been found. Stephen A. Gaskill was the son of Elijah Gaskill and Holland Roberts and brother to John W. Gaskill, father of Frank Gaskill (see numbers 15 and 16).

Elijah Gaskill was born about 1810 and married Holland Roberts who was born about 1810. They were married 15 February 1836 and had eight children: John W., Jane Ann, Joseph Earls, Winey, Mary C., Elijah T., Matilda, and Stephen A. Gaskill. Elijah Gaskill was a fisherman on Portsmouth as was Stephen.

Stephen A. Gaskill was born about 1850 and married Lydia A. Whitehurst, daughter of David W. Whitehurst and Sarah Manson. Stephen Gaskill and Lydia Whitehurst were married 24 April 1884. David Whitehurst and Sarah Manson were married 21 March 1833. Stephen was a fisherman, like the majority of men on Portsmouth. He is not listed in the 1880 Federal Census for Portsmouth Island and he and Lydia do not appear in the Census for Portsmouth Island after 1880, showing they had left the Island by the time of the 1900 Census. (There are no census records for 1890.)

76. Joe Dixon House and Store Site

Figure 104. Water Cistern to the Joe Dixon House, photograph by J. E. White.

Figure 105. Joe and Lorena Dixon, photograph courtesy of
Cape Lookout National Seashore Park.

This was the original site of the Dixon/Salter house (figure 6), built by Joe Dixon (figure 105) around 1900. Joe Dixon was a Freemason, and operated a store nearby. "He had most anything you wanted in his store. Food and hardware…he had the prettiest wash bowl and pitchers."[329] In addition to operating the store, Joe "used to fish pound nets."[330] He also owned a sharpie named *The Lorena Dee*.[331] Theodore Salter purchased the house and store from Joe Dixon about 1929 and moved the house to its current site in the village (See #7). All that is left of this site is the large square cistern (figure 104). The park service cut the hole in the cistern a number of years ago for safety purposes.

Figure 106. Dipping Vat, photograph by J. E. White.

77. Dipping Vat

Located about one-half way between the Joe Dixon house site and the Tom Gilgo, Sr. house site, is the dipping vat (figure 106). It was used to dip cattle and horses to keep the ticks off. It would be filled with chemicals and was used to immerse the animals to kill ticks and keep them off the animals. "Everyone was supposed to dip their livestock twice a year."[332] It was just deep enough "for a horse or a cow to go down in. It had an incline that went down in the vat and then they come out on the other side."[333]

Tour Directions

Follow the road back to the Straight Road. Just a short distance down the Straight Road on the left is the location of the Old School House or the Academy.

Figure 107. Old School House, photograph courtesy of Cape Lookout National Sea Shore Park.

78. The Old School House Site

The old school site is located on the left or east side of the Straight Road as it reaches the Middle Community. The road forks shortly after the school site to go into the Middle Community, or to continue on down the Straight Road to Gilgo Creek.

As early as 1805, there was a school or an academy located on Portsmouth as described by John Mayo. He described the academy as having a school for six months out of the year.[334] "In 1815, this building and 2 acres of land around it were set aside for the use of the academy."[335] In 1822, the academy was damaged by a hurricane as evidenced by an effort to raise the funds necessary to make repairs to it in December of that year.[336]

By 1860 there were only two teachers for the entire school: Miss Love Ireland (daughter of Earles Ireland), and Miss Margaret Mayo (daughter of Marcus Mayo).[337] Right in front of the academy was a large pond, called the "Academy Pond" and the clearing in front of the academy was the "Academy Green."[338] The Academy was located near the center of the island to make it convenient for children living at both ends of the island. The Academy was for paying students only and not a public school. Tuition was charged for each student who attended. When the new school was built around the later part of the 19th Century, the old Academy building became the Primitive Baptist Church.

The new school (figure 107) which was built in the later part of the 19th century, was wooden with ceilings that were 12 to 15 feet high.[339] "The building had wooden blinds, that was [sic] hinged- that would open. They were closed every night and opened every morning."[340] All grades were located in the one room school house, which was heated by a wood burning and later a coal burning stove. In 1917, there were 36 school children in attendance. The old school was replaced by the newer school house in the mid-1920s. The only visible relic of the old school house is the old safe (figure 108) which is still partially visible among the bushes and briars.

Figure 108. Photograph of the School Safe, courtesy of Michael Rikard, Cape Lookout National Sea Shore Park.

79. Primitive Baptist Church Site

The Primitive Baptist Church was located about three-fourths of a mile south of the old schoolhouse, across the Straight Road from Tom Gilgo, Sr.'s house and was located in the original Academy building.[341] At one time, it had a large congregation, but by the early 20th Century, it had only four or five members. The Gilgo family belonged to this church in the late 1800s and early 1900s. When Tom Gilgo married Sarah James Dixon, who was a member of the Methodist Church, the family began going to the Methodist Church. The hurricane of 1899 severely damaged the Primitive Baptist Church.[342] When that same hurricane destroyed the school house or academy, school was held here in the Primitive Baptist Church until the new school house could be built nearby. The hurricane of 1913 completely destroyed the church,[343] but there were too few active members at that time to rebuild it. The congregation only met about once every three months or so during the last few years of the church's existence.[344]

80. Bill Gilgo House Site

Located on the point near the sound is the site of the Gilgo home place. This is the site where Bill Gilgo and his wife Mahettable Wallace lived prior to the Civil War.[345] Bill Gilgo was the son of William and Sarah Gilgo who lived in the Straits area of Carteret County. William fought in the American Revolution as a British soldier. He died sometime before 1800 as Sarah is listed as a single mother with two sons: Bill Gilgo and his brother, Major Gilgo. In 1808 their mother died and both boys were bound out as "orphans." Bill was bound out to James Gaskill who lived in the Straits area and later lived on Portsmouth Island.

In 1823, James Gaskill sold his property on Portsmouth, house and land, to Bill Gilgo. This is the property located here. Bill Gilgo died in 1849 and his wife, Mahettable, died shortly after the Civil War.[346] There is a Mrs. Gilgo buried in Cedar Grove Cemetery in New Bern, North Carolina, who died 20 September 1867.[347]

(There is no proof that this Mrs. Gilgo is Mahettable Gilgo, but there is a good probability that it is she.)

Their son, William Gilgo, also called "Bill," continued to live at this site. Bill Gilgo had blue eyes, brown hair, was five feet eight and one half inches tall, and was one of the many pilots who operated from Portsmouth Island.[348] He served in the Civil War but ran away or deserted. "He and another feller ran away together. And they went out to look for um. I guess they would have killed um if they found them. They said that one of um, went up a chimney and stood on the pot hangers—up the chimney, you know they cooked in the fireplace in those days. This fellow, he searched the house, but didn't happen to look up the chimney. That's the only place he missed, they said. If they had caught em, he wood[sic] have cetched the devil. . . .That was in the time of the wars…He stayed, he didn't leave. He fell in with somebody."[349] According to Nina Mann Dixon, Bill Gilgo was impressed into the Federal or Union Army when the Yankees came through. (At this point, no record of William "Bill" Gilgo having been in either the Union or Confederate Service has been found.)

William "Bill" Gilgo married Emeline Robinson, daughter of James Robinson and Lovie Styron of Cedar Island.[350] Bill and Emeline Gilgo had eleven children: James Warren, George Wallis, William Thomas, Susan Jane, Anson, Angeline "Angie", Sarah, Lydia, Willis Monroe, Theressa, and Vera. They lived at this site until her death in 1902 and his in 1906.[351]

Figure 109. Photograph of William Thomas Gilgo, Sr.

81. Joe Roberts/Tom Gilgo House Site

This site was the original site of Joe Roberts' house. The house was extremely old and was most likely built by Daniel Heady in the early part of the 19th Century.

Daniel Heady purchased this lot from David Wallace on 18 April 1826. On 4 August 1828, he sold part of his property here to William W. Dixon for the sum of seventy five dollars, "containing Six Acres to be the same more or Less of the high ground."[352] In the deed, Heady mentions a house on the property. On 30 March 1837, Daniel Heady sold a parcel of property out of the same land he received from David Wallace, consisting of one acre of land, to Denard Roberts for the sum of twenty dollars.[353] Joseph Roberts received this property from his father, Denard Roberts.

Joe (Joseph) Roberts was born on Portsmouth about 1817. Around 1845 he married Betsy Gaskill, daughter of Joseph Gaskill and Mary Salter. They had two children, Denard Roberts (born around 1846) and Rebecca Roberts (born around 1850), and probably additional children as well. On 3 May 1866, Joe Roberts married a second time to Rebecca Ann Gooding. They had at least two children: James W. Roberts and Hannah Roberts. Joseph (Joe) Roberts was a pilot operating in Ocracoke Inlet.

Joseph and Rebecca's son, James Watson Roberts was born 6 April 1868. He purchased this house and site from his father, Joseph Roberts, "with all the buildings and improvements to thereon" for the sum of "twenty five Dollars" consisting of "fifty acres on which we now live."[354] He lived here with his wife, Susan Jane Gilgo, daughter of William Gilgo and Emeline Robinson, whom he married on 31 March 1890. James "Jim" Roberts was a commercial fisherman. They had five children: Ada, George, Steve, Verona and Alec. They lived in this house until 1910 when they left Portsmouth and moved to Belhaven, N. C. Shortly afterwards, they sold their house in Belhaven to Capt. Terrell, Commander of the Portsmouth Life Saving Station and moved to Morehead City, N. C. He purchased a house at 908 Bridges Street for $1,500 from R. T. Willis in August 1912, where they lived near other families who had moved from Portsmouth.

William Thomas Gilgo (figure 109), brother-in-law to Joseph Roberts, purchased this house and lot from Joe Roberts on 24 July 1919 "in consideration for one hundred and sixty five Dollars" consisting of a tract of land "estimated to be twelve acres."[355] Tom and his wife, Sarah James Dixon Gilgo had lived next door to Joe Roberts in a much smaller house. This was an opportunity for them to move in to a much larger house to accommodate their large family. Tom Gilgo and his wife, Sarah James Dixon, lived in this house until they moved to Oriental, N. C. in 1933 following the September hurricane. Tom and Sarah James, known to all as "Miss Jim," had five children: Lemmie, Blanche, Tom, Jr., James, and Elmo Gilgo. Sarah James Dixon, was the daughter of George Dixon and Emeline Salter of Portsmouth.

82. Tom Gilgo/Lemmie Gilgo House Site

There were three houses located in this general vicinity along the Straight Road near the bridge which crossed the creek over to Sheep Island.[356] The house closest to the creek was the Earles Ireland house, also known as the "Big House Place" and was sold to Sophronia Gilgo and her husband Warren Gilgo (#83). The house in the middle was the original Tom Gilgo, Sr. house and the house furtherest away from the creek was the Joe Roberts' house.[357] Tom Gilgo lived in the middle house until 1919 when he purchased the Joe Roberts' house and moved there.[358] When he did, his son Lemmie Gilgo and his wife, Louisa Spencer, of Ocracoke, moved in to this house. They were married January 30, 1918. He served in World War I.[359] (See number 71).

83. James Warren Gilgo House Site

This house site is one that goes back to the earliest part of Portsmouth's history and is located along Warren Gilgo's Creek on the north side of the creek between Sheep Island and the Middle Community. Earles Ireland purchased this site in 1841 and called it the "Big House Place,"[360] but no copy of the original deed has been found. In 1895, Sophronia Gilgo purchased the house from the heirs of Earles Ireland.[361] Sophronia Gilgo, daughter of Christopher Salter and Matilda Styron, had previously been married to George T. Salter. After his death, she married James Warren Gilgo (figure 110), son of William Gilgo and Emeline Robinson Gilgo.[362] There is a lot of debris located at this site, including the remains of an old engine that Warren Gilgo used as part of a fishing factory located at the site.

Warren and Sophronia, called "Pud," lived here until around the turn of the century, when they left Portsmouth and moved to Davis, N. C. They were living on Portsmouth during the 1900 census, but moved to Davis shortly thereafter.[363] They tore their house down that was located here and rebuilt it at Davis, along with a fish factory there. They remained in Davis where they died and are buried. They had two children: Goldie and Ruby.[364]

Figure 110. James Warren Gilgo

James Warren Gilgo was born 27 November 1866 and died on 7 December 1953. Sophronia Salter was born in 13 July 1862 and died 26 September 1942. Sophronia was married earlier to George T. Salter, son of William and Polly Salter (31 October 1883). She married James Warren Gilgo on 17 September 1888. In addition, a tombstone has been found in the creek, for a boy who was born to them and died very young.[365]

Figure 111. Grave Stone pulled out of Gilgo Creek, located in Community Cemetery, photograph by J. E. White.

84. Gilgo Cemetery

The Gilgo family cemetery is now located in Warren Gilgo Creek, on the north side, just off the banks. The cemetery is located approximately two-thirds up the creek from the mouth of the creek. All the tombstones are underwater, but several have been retrieved and placed on the banks during the past few years. Some of the tombstones can be read, while one is so smooth that it can not be read at all. These have now been removed and placed in the community cemetery in the village (figure 111).

Elizabeth Gilgo,
12 years old
daughter of William and Mahettable Wallace
Died: 1860s

Captain William Austin
Died: Aug 4, 1832 age 41 years
Masonic emblem

Figure 112. Warren Gilgo Creek, photograph by J. E. White.

85. Warren Gilgo Creek

Warren Gilgo Creek (figure 112), often called Sheep Island Slough, was named for Warren Gilgo, whose home was located on the northern side of the creek, approximately half way between the mouth of the creek and its source. Warren Gilgo fished and oystered as well as having a small shop or fish factory located here. The creek used to be rather small, crossable by a foot bridge which connected the Straight Road in the Middle Community to the community of Sheep Island.

Today, numerous hurricanes have washed through, making this creek as deep as six to eight feet in the center and at least one hundred yards or so wide. As it got deeper and wider, it engulfed the Gilgo family cemetery, totally covering it in three to five feet of water. To get from the north, or Middle Community side of the creek to the south, or Sheep Island side of the creek, one needs to travel by boat, or come up by road from the beach. As the Straight Road is cleaned up, perhaps it will be possible in the future to walk to the Creek and around the eastern end to Sheep Island.

Part III: Sheep Island

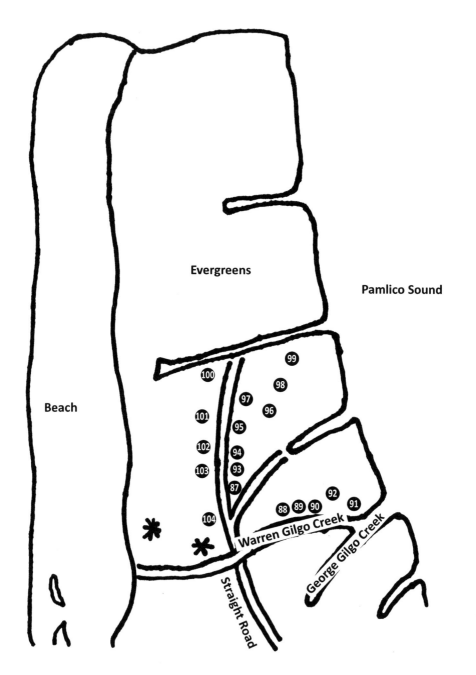

86. Sheep Island

The southern most inhabited part of Portsmouth Island is Sheep Island, which is located approximately three miles south of the Village. The land was noted for the numerous sheep located there in the late 1700s. This part of Portsmouth is separated from the rest of the island by Warren Gilgo's Creek, sometimes called Sheep Island Slough. Originally, this creek was neither very deep nor very wide, but numerous hurricanes washed through here, expanding both the width and depth of the creek. The creek used to be crossed by a foot bridge located near its source that was a continuation of the Straight Road which goes all the way to the end of Sheep Island, about a mile south of here. The only way to reach Sheep Island today is by boat.

In the late 1800s and early 1920s, there were numerous people living in this community. Among those living here were Sabra Roberts, James Gilgo, Manson Fulcher, and Cora Robinson. In addition, a number of fishing and hunting camps were located on this end of the island, including Tom Salter's Camp, the Battle Boys Camp, Ben Salter's Camp , and Ross Salter's Camp. Further south was the Pilentary Club House. All that is left standing on Sheep Island is the Ross Salter Camp, the Battle Boys Camp, and one cemetery which contains the grave of Governor John Wallace of Shell Castle and his wife, Rebecca.

Figure 113. John Wallace Salter House, photograph courtesy of Eula Pearl Williams Beauchamp, New Bern, N. C.

87. John Wallace Salter Home

This is the site of the Salter Camp, originally the Salter Gun Club. The original building was the old Salter homesite (figure 113), built by Ross Salter's parents, John Wallace Salter and Sidney Jane Styron. John Wallace Salter was born 15 August 1873, son of Christopher Thomas Salter born 4 July 1829 and his wife Matilda Styron born 4 June 1839 (figure 114).

John Wallace never went to school like the other children due to a heart defect when he was born. His father died when he was only 13 years old, leaving him and his brother Dave to take care of the family. He oystered, fished, and hunted for a living. He would dress and salt fish in kegs or barrels to take to Washington, N. C., to sell. In addition, he served as a hunting guide on the island. He had hunting blinds in the water and had live duck decoys, along with some that he had carved. He had livestock, horses, and cattle. He raised chickens, ducks, and enough hogs for his family to have which meant feeding, and slaughtering them. In addition, he had sheep at one time which he sheared and shipped the wool. After he married Sidney Jane Styron, she taught him to read and write.[366]

Figure 114. John Wallace Salter and Sidney Jane Styron, photograph courtesy of Eula Pearl Beauchamp, New Bern, N. C.

His home became known as the Salter Gun Club (Figure 115).[367] "The most noted hunter the family ever guided for was Babe Ruth."[368] John dismantled his home during the 1940s, and moved to Atlantic,[369] where he used the materials out of the original house to build his home there. He later moved to Atlantic, N. C. where he died 20 July 1950.

Figure 115. Ross Salter Camp, leased to Bobby Hill, photograph by J. E. White.

Figure 116. Ross Salter and Gladys Gaskill, photograph courtesy of Eula Pearl Williams Beauchamp.

Later, a hunting and fishing camp was built here by his son, Ross Salter (Figure 116). Today, the camp is leased by Bobby Hill of Morehead City.

Figure 117. Dave Salter, photograph courtesy of Pinkie Willis of New Bern, N. C.

88. Dave Salter

Dave Salter (figure 117), born 25 November 1868, was the son of Christopher Salter and Matilda Styron (daughter of Zachariah Styron and Martha "Patsey" Roberts), and brother to Sabra Salter Roberts. (Dave Salter was also brother to John Wallace Salter, Theodore Salter, and Sophronia "Pud" Salter who married Warren Gilgo). Dave Salter lived in the old Salter home place with his mother until she died.[370] The house originally belonged to Zachariah Styron.

The house was old when his parents (Christopher Salter and Matilda Styron) purchased it. It was told to me that herbs still hung from the exposed beams and rafters inside the house, left there when Indians lived there.[371] There was a brick cistern beside the house to catch the rain water from the roof.

Figure 118. Buella Bragg, photograph courtesy of Cape Lookout National Seashore Park.

Dave Salter continued to live in the house after his parents' death. He never married, but dated Buella Bragg (figure 118) for forty years. She was the daughter of Valentine Bragg and the sister of Tom Bragg. She spent most of her life taking care of her family as did he. When she was able to get married, he was busy taking care of his family members and when he was able to get married, she was taking care of her family members. When asked why didn't you get married? He told his niece Dot Salter Willis that when "she was ready I wasn't ready, and when I was ready, she wasn't ready."[372]

He loved to dance, often taking his niece over to Ocracoke to the square dances held there.[373] He went to every dance at Portsmouth, Ocracoke, and Beaufort and carried his dancing shoes with him everywhere he went. When he died, a lady there at his funeral, she knew him said, "Well, Dave Salter's dancing feet have stopped."[374]

He fished for a living, along with oystering and clamming. When his brother-in-law, Albert R. Roberts died, his sister Sabra James Roberts moved in with him, along with her two small children: Nora Roberts and Norwood Roberts. (Her home had been destroyed in a hurricane). Albert Roberts had run a fish boat when he was alive.[375] When Dave moved in with his sister, he became a "daddy" to her two small children, caring for them as he would his own. Nora Roberts married Harris Fulcher, who also lived on Sheep Island. After the 1933 hurricane, they left Portsmouth Island and moved to Oriental, North Carolina[376] where Mrs. Nora died in 2004 and is buried. Dave Salter moved to Cedar Island where he died of cancer in 1932[377] and is buried in the Lola Cemetery.

Figure 119. Albert Roberts House, photograph courtesy of Nora Roberts Fulcher, Oriental, N. C.

Albert Roberts' House Site

This house site (figure 119) was the home of Albert R. Roberts (figure 120), son of Denard R. and Bernasia F. Roberts. Albert Roberts was a fisherman on the island like most of the other men. This house was destroyed in a hurricane. He married Sabra Salter (figure 121), daughter of Christopher Salter and Matilda E. Styron. Albert was born in 1873 and Sabra was born in 1875. They had two children: Norwood and Nora. For more information on this family, see number 88. (Nora Roberts married Harris Fulcher and they had three children: Lucile, Lina, and Sabra Elizabeth "Pinkie" Fulcher.

Figure 120. Albert Roberts, photography courtesy of Pinkie Willis, New Bern, N. C.

Figure 121. Sabra James Salter Roberts, photograph courtesy of Nora Roberts Fulcher, Oriental, N. C.

90. Tom Roberts House Site

Eason Thomas "Tom" Roberts lived here next to his brother, Albert. He was born in 1875 and married Mamie Mason, daughter of W. R. & Francis Mason, 21 October 1899. Like his brother Albert, Tom fished and oystered for a living. In addition, Tom ran a small store on Sheep Island for a while.[378]

Figure 122. Jim and Martha Newton, photograph courtesy of Cape Lookout National Seashore Park.

91. James Newton

This area of Sheep Island is known as "Newton's Point" because of the Newton family who lived here in the latter half of the 19th century. The ruins of their house can be seen in the area and there is supposed to be a Newton Cemetery nearby, but that has yet to be found.

James S. Newton (figure 122) who lived here was the son of Joshua Newton. Joshua was listed as a pilot for the inlet, while James became a fisherman. By the time James Newton had reached adulthood, there were very few pilots left operating out of Ocracoke Inlet. The storms had shifted the major inlet northwards to Hatteras Inlet and the need for pilot services for Ocracoke Inlet steadily fell off after the 1844 hurricane. James was born about 1827. In 1850 he married Judith Simpson (bond 13 August 1850) and they had four children: Jesse, Bennett, Archibald, and Cora.

After Judith's death, James married Mary "Martha" E. Emery (bond 23 October 1865). James and Mary "Martha" had at least four children, William, Charles, Bennett, and William B. (Evidently, their son, William born about 1867 died because they had a second son which they named William B., who was born about 1879.) By the 1880 Federal Census, their son Jesse had married Vertie Unknown and they had two daughters: Martha and Mary C. Newton.

The Newtons must have died or left Portsmouth Island by 1900 because after the 1880 Federal Census, there is no further record of any Newtons left on Portsmouth.

Figure 123. Bill Robinson, Virginia Salter and David Salter, photograph courtesy of Eula Pearl Williams Beauchamp, New Bern, N. C.

92. Billy Robinson House Site

The Billy Robinson (figure 123) who lived here was the son of William Roberson (sic) and Rebekeah Willis,[379] who were married July 25, 1839.[380] In the 1850 Federal Census, William Roberson's occupation was given as "carpenter."[381] He had at least two children by Rebekeah: Emeline, who later married James Willis, and William Robinson, called "Billy." Rebekeah must have died in the early part of the 1850s, for on December 10, 1858, William Roberson married Catherine Davis.[382] By her, he had at least three children: Sparrow, Annie, and Cora. In the 1860 census, William listed his occupation as "Merchant." By the time of the 1870 census, Catherine is dead, with William in charge of the household. His occupation is now listed as "Mariner." William Roberson lived here until sometime after the 1880 census after which he died.

Billy Robinson, son of William and Rebekeah was living with his father in the 1870 census, unmarried, and gave his occupation as that of "fisherman." Though William Roberson is listed in the 1880 census, his son Billy is not. In fact, he doesn't show up again until the 1910 census where he is listed living on Sheep Island with his wife Sidney.[383] Sidney must have died by 1920, because she is no longer listed in the census. His sister Cora is listed as living with him on Sheep Island.

Figure 124. Ben Salter, photograph courtesy of Eula Pearl Williams Beauchamp.

93. Ben Salter

Benjamin Bowden Salter (figure 124), was born on Portsmouth Island on 30 June 1899, to John Wallace Salter and Sidney Styron Salter. He attended school on Portsmouth Island through the eighth grade. At the age of 15, he left the island and began working on the *S. S. Jamestown* with the Old Dominion Steamship Company in Norfolk, Virginia. In 1917, at the age of 18, he met and married Thelma Styron, daughter of William Reilly and Lydia Ann Emory Styron. They had six children: Ethel Marie, Doris Evelyn, Mary Elizabeth, Geraldine Farrar, Margaret Carolyn, and William Benjamin. Doris Evelyn was the only one of his children born on Portsmouth Island (and the last living person who was born on Portsmouth).

For a while he served in the US Coast Guard stationed in New York State. Later he was engaged in commercial fishing in Pamlico County. But for the most part of his life, he served as a commercial fisherman and guide for hunters based off of Portsmouth Island. While he lived on Portsmouth Island his home was located here on Sheep Island. After he left Sheep Island, he moved to Atlantic, N. C.[384] He sold his home to Cecil Gilgo who took what materials he could use from the house and built his own house near the school house. (See number 36.)

He and Thelma celebrated their fiftieth wedding anniversary on Sunday, July 16, 1967. Ben died 16 May 1983 and Thelma died 13 October 1992. Both are buried in the Atlantic Cemetery.

Figure 125 Jim Gilgo.

94. James Gilgo House Site

Located in this area, was James Monroe Gilgo's (Figure 125) house. He was the son of William Gilgo and Sarah James Dixon and was born in 1905. At the age of 13, he began working for his uncle, Will Dixon, as a cook and engineer for the North Carolina State Fisheries Commission.[385] Shortly after marrying Lucy Oglesby, daughter of John W. Oglesby of Morehead City in 1924, they moved to Morehead City where they lived until about 1940 when they moved to Washington, N. C. where he became an auto mechanic for Cox Motor Company and she became a nurse.[386] After his death in 1968, she moved in with her son Bill Gilgo who lived in New Bern.

95. John B. Styron House Site

This was the house site of John B. Styron and his wife Louisa. John B. Styron was the son of Zachariah Styron and Martha "Patsy" Roberts. John was born in 1846 and was a fisherman. After Louisa died, John Styron married Mary Ella Willis, daughter of George R. Willis and Mary Elizabeth "Beth" Salter. He oystered and fished for a living as did most of the men on Portsmouth. John Styron's mother lived here with them until her death.[387] They had five children: Charles H., George Washington Styron, Stephen, David, and Mary.

96. Steve Styron

Stephen Styron, son of John B. Styron, lived at this site, next to his father. Like his father, Stephen Styron was a fisherman. He married Alice Fulcher, daughter of Manson and Cassie Fulcher, on 10 September 1903. They had two children: John B. Styron and Gracie Styron.

97. George Mayo

The Mayo family had lived on Portsmouth Island since the late 1700s, with its founding father, John Mayo, living on Shell Castle Island in the 1800 Federal Census and who died in 1845. His son, John D. Mayo was born on Portsmouth, July 11, 1805 and married Susan Mason of Mattamuskeet in Hyde County, who was born February 10, 1802. They were married January 9, 1823 at Portsmouth. They had ten children: Sarah E. Mayo, born, November 4, 1824; Edward Mayo, born December 22, 1926; Warren Mayo, January 5, 1828; James Mayo, born June 5, 1830; Sidney Mayo, born September 26, 1833; Edward Mayo, born November 8, 1835; William Mayo, born October 19, 1837; Milton Mayo, born April 7, 1840; Benjamin F. Mayo, born August 28, 1842; and Mary Mayo, born April 25, 1845. All the children were born on Portsmouth Island. Edward Mayo who was born December 22, 1826 died March 12, 1827 and Mary Mayo died November 13, 1846. The rest of the children lived to adulthood.[388]

George R. Mayo was the son of Marcus and Barbara Mayo and was born about 1825. In the 1850 Federal Census, his occupation was given as "Mariner", while in the 1860 Federal Census, it was given as "Fisherman." George's wife, Margaret, was listed as a School Teacher in that same Federal Census. It appears that George's wife, Margaret, died early or at least by the 1870 Federal Census, when she no longer appears in the household. No Mayo is listed on Portsmouth Island after the 1880 Federal Census and George Mayo does not appear in the 1880 Federal Census for Portsmouth Island.

John D. Mayo died July 20, 1866 and his wife Susan Mayo died July 21, 1866.[389] George R. Mayo must have been the brother of John Mayo.

Figure 126. Gov. John Wallace Grave, photograph by J. E. White.

98. John Wallace Cemetery

The cemetery is probably larger than currently cleared. The most noted person buried within this cemetery is "Governor" John Wallace of Shell Castle (figure 126). John Wallace died in 1810 and his second wife, Rebecca, buried beside him, died in 1828. "Governor" Wallace's tombstone is a large marble one, fully engraved as follows:

Here is deposited the remains of Captain John Wallace Governor of Shell Castle, who departed this life July 22nd 1810. Age 52 Years 6 months.
Shell Castle Mourns;
Your pride is in the dust: Your boast, your glory in
The dreary grave, Your sun is set ne'er to illume again.
This sweet asylum from this Atlantic wave.
He's here beneath this monumental Tomb.
Thy awful gloom amid the silent dead.
Thy founder lies whose sainted soul we trust to heaven.
His mansion has its journey sped. Mourn,

> Charity benevolence
> Be wail. With one hospitality his lots deplore.
> His own with one unanimous acclaim. Misfortunes Son will
> View his like no more.[390]

Buried beside him is his second wife, Rebecca. She has a similar monument over her grave:

> **Rebecca Wallace**
> Born 11th. June 1771 Departed this life 22nd.
> November 1823
> She left this world with shining hope for a better.
> Leaving three daughters and two sons, bereaved by her death.[391]

Others buried in the cemetery include: Elizabeth Mayo, Eleazar Mayo, Sarah J. Babb, and Virginia S. Babb.[392]

Sarah J. Babb
b. September 28, 1896
d. October 6, 1896

Virginia S. Babb
b. December 16, 1906
d. January 30, 1907

Son of Milard & Rebecca Mayo
Eleazar
b. April 3, 1827
d. June 17, 1858

Figure 127. Salter-Battle Boys Camp, photograph by J. E. White.

99. Tom Salter/Battle Boys Camp

This is the site of a hunting camp established by the Battle Brothers (figure 127) of Mullins, South Carolina on land purchased from the Salters. The camp was run or occupied by Tom Salter. Tom lived here year round and had free use of the building and site. He, along with his brother Charlie Salter, hunted and fished for a living, and served as a hunting guide as well. In turn for his being able to use the place year round, whenever the Battle Brothers came to the island to hunt, he would serve as their hunting guide, as well as guide for their guests who came to the island. Tom first married Eula Ireland and then, Ada Salter. Tom and Ada had three children: Edward Roscoe, Rebecca Lauren, and Ellen Faye Salter. Ben Salter was usually at the camp when the Battle Brothers were on Portsmouth Island and helped them out as well. He later moved to Atlantic, N. C., where he died and is buried.

100. Billy Salter

Bill Salter's Creek was named after William W. Salter, who lived near the creek on the southern end of Sheep Island in the later half of the 1800s. William "Billy" Salter was the son of William Salter of Hunting Quarters (Atlantic), where he married Mary Unknown sometime around 1840. Throughout the various censuses taken in the 1800s, Billy Salter's occupation was listed as "fisherman."[393]

Bill and his wife, Mary "Polly," lived at Hunting Quarters until sometime between 1850 and 1860 when they moved to the upper end of Portsmouth Island, in the middle of the village.[394] In 1862, their daughter Emeline Salter married George S. Dixon, son of William C. Dixon, Jr.[395] By the time of the 1870 census, the Salters had moved to the lower or southern end of Sheep Island.[396]

During the Civil War, Federal soldiers would go out on the island to capture a cow to take back to camp and butcher. The people of Portsmouth would allow their cows to wander about the island to feed on the grasses and shrubs growing throughout the island. Polly Salter was determined that no "Damn Yankee" was going to steal her cow. So she went out, got her cow, and carried it inside the house at night so they couldn't steal it. Billy and Polly Salter resided here until their deaths in the 1880s. Both Billy and Polly are buried in the community cemetery at Atlantic, North Carolina, as is their daughter Emeline Salter Dixon.[397]

Figure 128. Manson & Crissie Fulcher, photograph courtesy of Dot Salter Willis.

101. William Manson Fulcher House Site

William Manson Fulcher (figure 128) was the son of John and Fannie Fucher. John and Fannie Fulcher were married 18 October 1882 at Hatteras in Dare County, NC. William married Elva Christian Midgett, daughter of Annie Midgette of Hatteras. William and "Crissie" moved to Portsmouth sometime before 1910, but why they moved to Portsmouth is unknown.

William Manson Fulcher was born 24 May 1856 and he died 7 January 1924. William's wife was Elva Christian Midgett but was always called "Chrissie." She was born 17 February 1862 at Hatteras and died 5 July 1945. Both are buried at Hatteras.

William Manson Fulcher was a commercial fisherman and "could pray the greatest prayers I've ever heard in my life. Make the hair stand right up."[398] "Chrissie" served as the Island's midwife.[399] They had eleven children: Claughton, Edward, James Harris (who married Nora Roberts, see number 88), Fannie, Alladin, Jerome, John, Levin, Alice, William, and Job.[400]

After Manson Fulcher died in 1924, Crissie remarried and she moved back to Hatteras where she died. Her marriage certificate to Manson Fulcher listed her last name as Holt, indicating that she probably had married prior to marrying Manson Fulcher.

102. Ed & Kate Styron House Site

This is the original site of the Ed and Kate Styron house. The house was built in 1933 just before the September hurricanes of that year. By 1934, nearly everyone on Sheep Island had left, as well as most of the people in the Middle Community. Kate didn't want to be left alone on Sheep Island, she wanted to be closer to the other people on Portsmouth. So, Ed dismantled the house and moved it to the Village near the Dixon/Babbs Cemetery where it is currently located. (See number 53.)

103. George Riley Willis House Site

George R. Willis, born 12 March 1859, was the son of George Willis and Sarah Mason. He married Mary Elizabeth Salter, born 7 August 1865, daughter of Christopher Thomas Salter and Matilda E. Styron. He was a fisherman and lived at this location until later moving the house into the village. (See number 44). In addition to fishing and oystering, he substituted as a crewman at the Lifesaving/Coast Guard Station.[401] They had two children: Clayton Willis and Mary Ella Willis, who married John Styron.[402] Later he moved his house to the village. George R. Willis died 27 November 1936 and Mary Elizabeth Salter Willis died 11 August 1954. (See number 58.)

Figure 129. Captain John Hill Home, Beaufort, N. C., photograph by J. E. White.

104. Captain John Hill House

Located somewhere on Sheep Island was the Captain John Hill house. Captain John Hill was the son of Peter Hill II and Sidney Rose and was born 2 July 1817 and died 2 May 1879. He was married four times: Elizabeth Willis, N. Elizabeth Unknown, Pennsylvania Rose, and Sarah Ann Smith according to Maxine Hill Olsen, Researcher. In 1850, he was living in Hunting Quarters but by 1860, they were living on Portsmouth Island. He served as Postmaster at Portsmouth between 27 February 1868 and October 22, 1869. Sometime after the 1870 census, he moved his home from Portsmouth Island "where it had stood for 100 years" to Beaufort, N. C. The house (figure 129) was loaded on a barge and moved to Beaufort where it stood for another 100 years before it was moved to its present location."[403]

Figure 130. Pilentary Club House, photograph courtesy of Cape Lookout National Seashore Park.

105. Pilentary Club House

Approximately ten miles up the banks from Portsmouth Village, which is to say, ten miles south of the Village, was located the Pilentary Club House (figure 130). Originally it could be reached by traveling from the Straight Road at its end on Sheep Island down a path or road to the Club, or along the beach. Today, the only way to reach the site is by the beach or by water.

The Pilentary Club was established by Theodore Rogers who began purchasing land in the area for the Mason family in 1885. He named the club after the Pilentary Tree.[404] The club was purchased in 1904 by Arthur Kemp, who resold it in 1905 to Jordan L. Mott, III who turned it into the club it is remembered for.[405] The building was completed in 1907 and "had fireplaces on both floors; wood was used for heating, coal for cooking. Two large concrete cisterns caught water drained from the roof…A fancy water closet (toilet), three large bedrooms and a maid's room were on the second floor…Other structures on the premises included two caretakers homes, a long, narrow, wood and coal shed, and a boat house. A picket fence extended around the club house, and a large flag pole rose in front of the club."[406]

Figure 131. President Franklin Roosevelt hunting at the Pilentary Club House, photograph courtesy of Cape Lookout National Seashore Park.

Under Jordan Mott's leadership, the Club became a center of social life. Many important guests were entertained here including Jim Goins, Arthur Duane, and Franklin D. Roosevelt (figure 131) while he served as Secretary of the Navy.[407] Alvin and Amelia Mason served as caretakers of the Pilentary Club in the late 1920s and early 1930s. John and Ina Salter served as caretakers after they left, and were caretakers when the hurricane hit in September 1933, destroying it. Joe Abbott served as chief cook at the Club for many years.

Figure 132 Morris Marina, "Kabin Kamps" photograph by J. E. White.

106. Morris Marina, "Kabin Kamps", and Ferry Service

Approximately twenty miles south of the Village are a number of cabins available for rent, year round for fishing, hunting, etc. These camps (Kamps) (figure 132) consist of a number of octagon shaped structures which will sleep up to six people. The "Kabins" have bunk beds, gas cooking stoves, heaters, hot water, and complete bathroom facilities.

In addition, there is ferry service from here to Atlantic, N. C. The ferry runs three times daily to and from Atlantic, and is capable of transporting two, four-wheel drive vehicles as well as walking passengers. For more information, contact Morris Marina at (252) 225-4261.

ENDNOTES

[1] Lionel Gilgo, Interview with Jim Godwin, Portsmouth, North Carolina, 15 July 1978.

[2] Steve Roberts, Interview with William Mansfield, Portsmouth, North Carolina, 3 September 1982.

[3] Southy J. Rew, Deed to Richard Casey. Carteret County Register of Deeds, Beaufort, N. C.: Book O, p. 54, 21 October 1797.

[4] Sarah McCulloh Lemmon, *Frustrated Patriots: North Carolina and the War of 1812* (Chapel Hill, N. C.: The University of North Carolina Press, 1973), 131-132.

[5] *Ibid.*

[6] *Ibid.*

[7] Sarah Olson, *Historic Resource Study, Portsmouth Village, Cape Lookout National Seashore, N. C.* (Denver, CO: United States Department of the Interior, National Park Service, March 1982), 61.

[8] R. Edward Earll, *North Carolina and Its Fisheries*, Part XII, n.d.

[9] Ben B. Salter. *Portsmouth Island: Short Stories and History* (Privately Published, 1972), 12.

[10] Elma Morgan Dixon, Interview with Nancy Godwin and Rebecca Harriett, Beaufort, North Carolina, 18 August 1979.

[11] Jerry Allegood. "Researchers dive into history in Ocracoke Inlet," Raleigh, North Carolina: *The News and Observer*, 13 May 1995.

[12] "Notes from Shell Castle," *The Mail Boat* (Harkers Island, N. C.: Spring, 1992, Vol 3, No.1), 4.

[13] *Ibid.*

[14] *Ibid.*

[15] Sonny Williamson. *Unsung Heroes of the Surf: The Lifesaving Service of Carteret County* (Marshallberg, N. C.: Grandma Publications, 1992), 77.

[16] Fred M. Mallison, The Civil War on the Outer Banks: A History of the Late Rebellion Along the Coast of North Carolina From Carteret to Currituck (Jefferson, N. C.: McFarland & Company, Inc., Publishers, 1998), 13.

[17] Allegood, "Researchers Diver into History."

[18] *Ibid.*

[19] Ellen Fucher Cloud, *Portsmouth: The Way it Was* (Ocracoke, N. C.: Live Oak Publications, 1996), 41.

[20] Connie Mason, "Timeline Portsmouth and Nearby Islands, *The Mailboat* (Harkers Island, N. C.: Spring 1992, Vol. 3, no. 1), 5.

21 Burke, *History of Portsmouth Island*, 29.
22 *Ibid.*, 33.
23 Olson, "Historic Resource Study, Portsmouth Village," 85.
24 Burke, *History of Portsmouth Island*, 43.
25 Olson, "Historic Resource Study, Portsmouth Village," 86.
26 Salter, *Portsmouth Island: Short Stories and History*, 26.
27 "Portsmouth Historic Zone Base Map," Washington, D.C.: United States Department of Interior, National Park Service, Cape Lookout National Seashore, n.d.
28 Lionel Gilgo, Interview with Jim Godwin, Portsmouth, North Carolina, 15 July 1978.
29 Steve Roberts, Interview with William Mansfield, Morehead City, North Carolina, 9 July 1982.
30 *Ibid.*, 9 July 1982.
31 *Ibid.*
32 *Ibid.*
33 Elma Morgan Dixon, Interview with Nancy Godwin and Rebecca Harriett, Beaufort, N. C., 18 August 1979.
34 Lionel Gilgo, Interview with Cat Troutman, Portsmouth, 24 September 1981.
35 Jack Dudley, *Carteret Waterfowl Heritage* (Morehead City, N. C.: Decoy Magazine, 409 North 35th Street, 1993), 56.
36 Lynn Salsi and Frances Eubanks, *The Crystal Coast* (Charleston, S.C.: Arcadia Publishing, 2000), 78.
37 Bedwell, *Portsmouth: Island With a Soul*, 38.
38 Elma Morgan Dixon, Interview with Nancy Godwin and Rebecca Harriett, Beaufort, N. C.: 18 August 1979.
39 Steve Roberts, Interview with William Mansfield, Morehead City, N. C.: 9 July 1982.
40 Salter, *Portsmouth Island: Short Stories and History*, 40-41.
41 Salsi and Eubanks, *The Crystal Coast*, 77.
42 Marian Gray Babb, Interview with Nancy Godwin, 26 July 1978.
43 *Ibid.*
44 Lionel Gilgo and Emma Gilgo, interview with William Mansfield, Atlantic, N. C., 7 July 1982.
45 Salsi and Eubanks, *The Crystal Coast*, 77.
46 Portsmouth Historic Zone Base Map.
47 Salter, *Portsmouth Island: Short Stories and History*, 55.

[48] Lionel Gilgo and Emma Gilgo, Interview with William Mansfield, Atlantic, N. C., 7 July 1982.

[49] "Historic Property Leasing Program," Cape Lookout National Seashore, Request for Proposals, Portsmouth Village," 1992, Appendix B, 1.

[50] Sarah Roberts Styron, Interview with Nancy Godwin, Beaufort, N. C., 31 December 1978.

[51] *Ibid.*

[52] *Ibid.*

[53] White, *The Gilgoes of Portsmouth Island and Related Familes*, 80.

[54] Salter, *Portsmouth Island: Short Stories and History*, 41.

[55] Steve Roberts, Interview with William Mansfield, Morehead City, N. C., 9 July 1982.

[56] Marian Gray Babb, Interview with Nancy Godwin, 26 July 1978.

[57] Karen Dugan, Notes on Portsmouth Island, Harkers Island, N. C.: Cape Lookout National Seashore Park, n.d.

[58] Lionel Gilgo and Emma Gilgo, Interview with William Mansfield, Atlantic, N. C., 7 July 1982.

[59] Portsmouth Historic Zone Base Map.

[60] *The Mailboat*, vol. 3, No. 1, 12.

[61] Bedwell, 87.

[62] Nina Mann Dixon, Interview with the author, Oriental, N. C., Winter/Spring, 1976.

[63] *Ibid.*

[64] Carteret County Register of Deeds, Beaufort, N. C., book W, p. 379, 22 April 1835.

[65] *Ibid.*

[66] Carteret County Register of Deeds, Beaufort, N. C., book WW, p. 550, 7 November 1901.

[67] *Ibid.*

[68] Carteret County Register of Deeds, Beaufort, N. C., book 4, p. 59, 29 September 1904.

[69] Nina Mann Dixon, Interview with the author, Oriental, N. C., Winter/Spring, 1976.

[70] Bedwell, *Portsmouth: Island With a Soul*, 28.

[71] Lionel Gilgo, Interview with Jim Godwin, Portsmouth, 15 July 1978.

[72] Portsmouth Historic Zone Base Map.

[73] Bedwell, *Portsmouth: Island With a Soul*, 28.

[74] *Ibid.*

[75] Marian Gray Babb, Interview with Nancy Godwin, 26 July 1978.
[76] Lionel Gilgo, Interview with Cat Troutman, Portsmouth, 24 September 1981.
[77] Portsmouth Historic Zone Base Map.
[78] Marian Gray Babb, Interview with Nancy Godwin, 26 July 1978.
[79] Dot Salter, Interview with the Author, Morehead City, North Carolina, 3 August 1996.
[80] Steve Roberts, Interview with William Mansfield, Portsmouth, 3 September 1982.
[81] Sherry White. "When life was young in a village called Portsmouth." *The News-Times*, 9 June 1995.
[82] Elma Morgan Dixon, Interview with Nancy Godwin, Beaufort, N. C.: 18 August 1979.
[83] *The Mailboat*, Spring 1992, Vol. 3, no. 1, 11.
[84] Cecil Gilgo and Iona Gilgo, Interview with Connie Mason, Davis, N. C., 8 March, 1985.
[85] Salter, *Portsmouth Island: Short Stories and History*, 19.
[86] Ruth Barbour, "Portsmouth Won't be the Same," *Carteret County News-Times* (18 January 1971).
[87] Carteret County Death Certificates, Beaufort, North Carolina: Register of Deeds Office, Vol 12, p. 187.
[88] Salter, *Portsmouth Island: Short Stories and History,* 21.
[89] Louie Dixon, Interview with Don Davis, et. al., 10 January 1978.
[90] Bedwell, *Portsmouth: Island With a Soul*, 43.
[91] Lionel Gilgo, interview with Jim Godwin, Portsmouth, 15 July 1978.
[92] *Ibid*.
[93] Steve Roberts, Interview with William Mansfield, Morehead City, N. C., 30 July 1982.
[94] *Ibid*.
[95] *Ibid*.
[96] Lionel Gilgo, Interview with Jim Godwin, Portsmouth, 15 July 1978.
[97] *Ibid*.
[98] Craven County Marriage License, Register of Deeds Office, book 3, page 380, 19 February 1870.
[99] Eula Pearl Beauchamp and Jo Ann Ernul Murphy, *Addendum, Cedar Grove Cemetery (oldest part),* New Bern, N. C. (privately printed, n.d.), 329.
[100] Bedwell, *Portsmouth: Island With a Soul*, 44.
[101] Dudley, *Carteret Waterfowl Heritage*, 55.

[102] Bedwell, *Portsmouth: Island With a Soul*, 44.

[103] Carteret County Register of Deeds, Beaufort, N. C.: book CC, p. 102, 3 April 1867.

[104] *Ibid.*

[105] Carteret County Register of Deeds, Beaufort, N. C.: book UU, p. 387, 20 August 1898.

[106] Carteret County Register of Deeds, Beaufort, N. C.: book ZZ, pp.34-35, 23 November 1898.

[107] Ben Salter, Interview, 10 January 1978.

[108] Ben Salter, *Portsmouth Island: Short Stories and History*, (Privately published, 1972), 42.

[109] Lionel Gilgo, Interview with Jim Godwin, Portsmouth Island, 17 July 1978.

[110] *Ibid.*

[111] Salter, *Portsmouth Island: Short Stories and History*, 59.

[112] Elma Morgan Dixon, Interview with Nancy Godwin and Rebecca Harriett, Beaufort, N. C., 18 August 1979.

[113] Portsmouth Historic Zone Base Map.

[114] Dot Salter Willis & Ben B. Salter, *Portsmouth Island: Short Stories & History* (Privately Published, 2004), 42.

[115] Dudley, *Carteret Waterfowl Heritage*, 42.

[116] *Ibid.*

[117] Lionel Gilgo and Emma Gilgo, Interview with William Mansfield, Atlantic, N. C., 7 July 1982.

[118] Steve Roberts, Interview with William Mansfield, Portsmouth, 3 September 1982.

[119] Dudley, *Carteret Waterfowl Heritage*, 52.

[120] Bedwell, Portsmouth: Island With a Soul, 42.

[121] Carteret County Register of Deeds, Beaufort, N. C.: book CC, p. 181, 17 September 1866.

[122] Carteret County Register of Deeds, Beaufort, N. C.: book CC, p. 180, 10 July 1857.

[123] *Ibid.*

[124] Eula Pearl Beauchamp, JoAnn Ernul Murphy, and Jerline (Jeri) S. Wetherington, *Craven County, North Carolina Cemeteries Volume 1, City of New Bern* (New Bern, N. C.: The Eastern North Carolina Genealogical Society, n.d.), 140.

[125] *New Bern Weekly Journal*, 21 July 1899, p. 4.

[126] *Ibid.*

[127] Carteret County Register of Deeds, Beaufort, N. C.: book CC, p. 26.

[128] *New Bern Daily Times*, 11 October 1871, p. 1.

[129] *New Bern Weekly Journal*, 21 July 1899, p. 4.

[130] Eula Pearl Beauchamp, JoAnn Ernul Murphy, and Jerline (Jeri) S. Wetherington, *Craven County, North Carolina Cemeteries Volume 1, City of New Bern (New Bern, N. C.:* The Eastern North Carolina Genealogical Society, n.d.), 140.

[131] Cloud, *Federal Censuses for 1850, 1860, 1870, 1880, 1900.*

[132] Steven Roberts, Interview with William Mansfield, Portsmouth, 3 September 1982.

[133] Carteret County Register of Deeds Office, Beaufort, N. C.: book U, pp. 9-10, 18 April 1826.

[134] Carteret County Register of Deeds Office, Beaufort, N. C.: book Y, p. 134, 20 April 1840.

[135] Carteret County Register of Deeds Office, Beaufort, N. C.: book MM, p. 390, 9 November 1884.

[136] Marian Gray Babb, Interview with Nancy Godwin, 26 July 1978.

[137] *Ibid.*

[138] Louie Dixon, Interview with Don Davis, et. al., 10 January 1978.

[139] Steven Roberts, Interview with William Mansfield, Portsmouth, 3 September 1982.

[140] Thompson, John L. and Lionel Gilgo, Cape Lookout National Seashore Document Number 559, Keeler Cemetery, Portsmouth Village, N. C., ca., 1980.

[141] Federal Census of the United States, 1860: Wallingford, New Haven, Connecticut, Roll: M653_84, p. 401.

[142] *New Bern Daily Journal*, 20 January 1885, p. 1.

[143] Carteret County Register of Deeds, Beaufort, N. C.: book T, pp. 128-129, 13 January 1824.

[144] Carteret County Register of Deeds, Beaufort, N. C.: book U, pp. 415, 8 August 1828.

[145] Federal Census of the United States, 1860, Wallingford, New Haven, Connecticut, Roll: M653_84, p. 401.

[146] Civil War Soldiers & Sailors System, http://www.civilwar.nps.gov/cwss/Personz_Detail.cfm (Charles B. Keeler).

[147] Craven County Register of Deeds, New Bern, N. C. (Volume 1, p. 80), 29 January 1865.

[148] Eula Pearl Beauchamp and Jo Ann Ernul Murphy, *1860 Census of Craven County, North Carolina* (Privately published, n.d.).

[149] Tombstone, Cedar Grove Cemetery, New Bern, North Carolina.

[150] Carteret County Register of Deeds, Beaufort, N. C.: book LL, p. 53, 13 January 1883.

[151] *New Bern Daily Journal*, 20 January 1885, p. 1.

[152] Dot Salter Willis and Ben B. Salter, *Portsmouth Island: Short Stories, History,* Edited by Frances A. Eubanks and Lynn S. Saisi, (Privately Printed, 2004), p. 60.

[153] *New Bern Weekly Journal,* 17 October 1905, p. 4.

[154] Craven County Register of Deeds, New Bern, N. C. Death Certificate, #22883.

[155] Eula Pearl Beauchamp, JoAnn Ernul Murphy, and Jerline (Jeri) S. Wetherington, *Craven County, North Carolina Cemeteries Volume 1 City of New Bern* (New Bern, N. C.: Eastern North Carolina Genealogical Society, n.d.), 52.

[156] Carteret County Register of Deeds, Beaufort, N. C.: book 6, p. 297, 11 December 1907.

[157] Lionel Gilgo and Emma Gilgo, Interview with William Mansfield, Atlantic, N. C., 1982.

[158] Lionel Gilgo, Interview with Jim Godwin, Portsmouth, 15 July 1978.

[159] *Ibid.*

[160] Salter, *Portsmouth Island: Short Stories and History*, 55.

[161] Lionel Gilgo, Interview with Jim Godwin, Portsmouth, 15 July 1978.

[162] Karen Dugan, Notes on Portsmouth Island, Cape Lookout National Seashore Park, n.d.

[163] Dot Salter, Interview with Jim Godwin, Portsmouth, 15 July 1978.

[164] "Historic Property Leasing Program—Request for Proposals," 1992.

[165] Burke, *History of Portsmouth Island*, 72.

[166] White, *The Gilgoes of Portsmouth Island and Related Families*, 63.

[167] *Ibid.*

[168] Carteret County Register of Deeds, book 9, p. 410, 15 July 1910.

[169] Carteret County Register of Deeds, book U, p. 415 (1828).

[170] Carteret County Register of Deeds, book LL, p. 53 (1883).

[171] Carteret County Register of Deeds, book 6, p. 297 (1907).

[172] Carteret County Register of Deeds, book 9, p. 410 (1910).

[173] Carteret County Register of Deeds, book 9, p. 410, 15 July 1910.

[174] Cecil Gilgo and Leona Gilgo, Interview with Connie Mason, Davis, N. C.: 8 March 1985.

[175] *Ibid.*

[176] Lionel Gilgo and Emma Gilgo, Interview with William Mansfield, Atlantic, N. C.: 1982.

[177] Bedwell, *Portsmouth: Island With a Soul*, 41.

[178] Lionel Gilgo and Emma Gilgo, Interview with William Mansfield, Atlantic, N. C.: 1982.

[179] Marian Gray Babb and Clara Salter Gaskins, Interview with Nancy Godwin, 9 August 1979.

[180] Interview with Lucy Beacham Gilgo, wife of Tom Gilgo, Jr., and the author, Oriental, N. C., 1980.

[181] Portsmouth Historic Zone Base Map.

[182] Elma Morgan Dixon, Interview with Nancy Godwin and Rebecca Harriett, Beaufort, N. C., 18 August 1979.

[183] Samuel and Susan Dudley. Deed to Trustees of Portsmouth Methodist Church, Carteret County Register of Deeds, book Y, p. 50-51, 7 March 1840.

[184] Salter, *Portsmouth Island: Short Stories and History,* 35.

[185] *Ibid.*

[186] *Ibid.*

[187] Elma Morgan Dixon, Interview with Nancy Godwin and Rebecca Harriett, Beaufort, N. C., 18 August 1979.

[188] *Ibid.*

[189] Marian Gray Babb, Interview with Nancy Godwin, 26 July 1978.

[190] Williamson, 80.

[191] Marian Gray Babb, Interview with Nancy Godwin, 26 July 1978.

[192] Lionel Gilgo, Interview with Jim Godwin, 26 July 1978.

[193] Salter, *Portsmouth Island: Short Stories and History,* 37.

[194] Sarah Roberts Styron, Interview with Nancy Godwin, Beaufort, N. C., 31 December 1978.

[195] *Ibid.*

[196] Portsmouth Historic Zone Map.

[197] Ben Salter, Interview, 10 January 1978

[198] Ellen Marie Cloud, Interview, July 2009

[199] Lionel Gilgo, Interview with Jim Godwin, Portsmouth, 15 July 1978.

[200] Elma Morgan Dixon, Interview with Nancy Godwin and Rebecca Harriett, Beaufort, 18 August 1979.

[201] Dudley, *Carteret Waterfowl Heritage,* 56.

[202] Lionel Gilgo, Interview with Jim Godwin, Portsmouth, 15 July 1978.

[203] Marian Gray Babb, Interview with Nancy Godwin, 26 July 1978.

[204] Elma Morgan Dixon, Interview with Nancy Godwin and Rebecca Harriett, Beaufort, 18 August 1979.

[205] Salter, *Portsmouth Island: Short Stories and History,* 57.

[206] Morgan Dickerman, Dudley family papers, Wilson, North Carolina.

[207] *Ibid.*

[208] Interview with Ellen Marie Cloud, July 2009.

[209] Ellen Fuclcher Cloud, *Portsmouth: The Way it Was*, 9-10.

[210] Lionel Gilgo and Emma Gilgo, Interview with William Mansfield, Atlantic, N. C.: 16 June 1982.

[211] F. Ross Holland, Jr., "A Survey Historty of Cape Lookout National Seashore," 44.

[212] Salter, *Portsmouth Island: Short Stories and History,* 35.

[213] Tombstone of Dr. Samuel Dudley, recorded by the author, Cedar Grove Cemetery, New Bern, N. C.

[214] Carteret County Clerk of Court, Wills, Will of Almira Dudley, 25 May 1916.

[215] Cedar Grove Cemetery, New Bern, North Carolina.

[216] Louie Dixon, Interview with Don Davis, et. al., 10 January 1978.

[217] Marian Gray Babb and Clara Salter Gaskins, Interview with Nancy Godwin, 9 August 1979.

[218] Lionel Gilgo, Interview with Jim Godwin, Portsmouth, 15 July 1978.

[219] *Ibid.*

[220] Nina Mann Dixon, Interview with the Author, Oriental, N. C.: 2 February, 1977.

[221] Ellen Fulcher Cloud, *The Federal Census of Portsmouth Island, N. C.*, Ocracoke, N. C.: Live Oak Publications, n.d.

[222] *Ibid.*

[223] *Ibid.*

[224] *Ibid.*

[225] *Ibid.*

[226] Lionel Gilgo and Emma Gilgo, Interview with William Mansfield, Atlantic, N. C.: 7 July, 1982.

[227] *Ibid.*

[228] Marian Gray Babbs, Interview with Nancy Godwin, 26 July 1978.

[229] Dudly, *Carteret Waterfowl Heritage*, 56-57.

[230] *Ibid.*

[231] Lionel Gilgo, Interview with Cat Troutman, Portsmouth, 24 September 1981.

[232] *Ibid.*

[233] Lionel Gilgo, Interview with Jim Godwin, Portsmouth, 15 July 1978.

[234] Nora Fulcher, Interview with William Mansfield, Oriental, N. C., 30 June 1982.

[235] Lionel Gilgo, Interview with Jim Godwin, Portsmouth, 15 July 1978.

[236] Lionel Gilgo and Emma Gilgo, Interview with William Mansfield, Atlantic, N. C., 16 June 1982.

[237] Portsmouth Historic Zone Map.

[238] Lionel Gilgo and Emma Gilgo, Interview, 16 June 1982.

[239] *Ibid.*

[240] *Ibid.*

[241] Louie Dixon, Interview with Don Davis, et. al., 10 January 1978.

[242] Marian Gray Babb, Interview with Nancy Godwin, 26 July 1978.

[243] Lionel Gilgo, Interview with Jim Godwin, Portsmouth, N. C., 15 July 1978.

[244] Marian Gray Babb, Interview with Nancy Godwin, Portsmouth, N. C., 26 July 1978.

[245] Steve Roberts, Interview with William Mansfield, Morehead City, N. C., 30 July 1982.

[246] Lionel Gilgo, Interview with Jim Godwin Portsmouth, N. C., 15 July 1978.

[247] Salter, *Portsmouth Island: Short Stories and History*, 51.

[248] Portsmouth Historic Zone Map.

[249] Marian Gray Babb, Interview with Nancy Godwin, Portsmouth, N. C., 26 July 1978.

[250] Nina Mann Dixon, Interview with the author, Oriental, N. C., 2 February 1977.

[251] Elma Morgan Dixon, Interview with Nancy Godwin and Rebecca Harriett, Beaufort, N. C., 18 August 1979.

[252] *Ibid.*

[253] Lionel Gilgo and Emma Gilgo, Interview with William Mansfield, Atlantic, N. C., 1982.

[254] Steve Roberts, Interview with William Mansfield, Morehead City, N. C., 9 July 1982.

[255] Lionel Gilgo and Emma Gilgo, Interview with William Mansfield, Atlantic, N. C., 17 July 1982.

[256] Dudley, *Carteret Waterfowl Heritage*, 56.

[257] Elma Morgan Dixon, Interview with Nancy Godwin and Rebecca Harriett, Beaufort, N. C., 18 August 1979.

[258] Ben Salter, Interview, 10 January 1978.

259 Elma Morgan Dixon, Interview with Nancy Godwin, Beaufort, N. C.: 18 August 1979.

260 Lionel Gilgo and Ethel Gilgo, Interview with William Mansfield, Cape Lookout National Seashore Park, 07 July 1982.

261 Karen Duggan, Notes on Portsmouth, Cape Lookout National Seashore Park, n.d.

262 *Ibid.*

263 Carteret County Register of Deeds, Beaufort, NC (TT, p. 528), 15 February, 1897.

264 Carteret County Register of Deeds, Beaufort, NC (UU, pg. 303), 6 September, 1897.

265 Karen Duggan, Notes on Portsmouth, Cape Lookout National Seashore Park, n.d.

266 *Ibid.*

267 *Ibid.*

268 *Ibid.*

269 Lionel and Emma Gilgo, Interview with William Mansfield, Atlantic, NC, 7 July 1982

270 Marian Gray Babb, Interview with Nancy Godwin, 26 July 1978.

271 Lionel & Emma Gilgo, Interview with William Mansfield, Atlantic, NC, 16 June 1982.

272 Lionel Gilgo, Interview with Jim Godwin, Portsmouth Island, 17 July 1978.

273 Steve Roberts, Interview with William Mansfield, Morehead City, NC, 9 July 1983.

274 Karen Duggan, Notes on Portsmouth, Cape Lookout National Seashore Park, n.d.

275 *Ibid.*

276 *Ibid.*

277 Portsmouth Historic Zone Base Map.

278 Marian Gray Babb, Interview with Nancy Godwin, 26 July 1978.

279 Ben Salter, Interview, 10 January 1978.

280 Steve Roberts and Clayton Willis, Interview with William Mansfield, Atlantic, N. C., 3 August 1982.

281 Lionel Gilgo, Interview with Jim Godwin, Portsmouth, N. C., 15 July 1978.

282 Steve Roberts and Clayton Willis, Interview with William Mansfield, Atlantic, N. C., 3, August 1982.

283 Portsmouth Historic Zone Base Map.

[284] Lionel Gilgo and Emma Gilgo, Interview with William Mansfield, Atlantic, N. C., 16 June 1982.

[285] Lionel Gilgo, Interview with Jim Godwin, Portsmouth, N. C., 15 July 1978.

[286] Salter, *Portsmouth Island: Short Stories and History*, 41.

[287] Karen Dugan, Notes on Portsmouth, Cape Lookout National Seashore Park, n.d.

[288] Ibid.

[289] Portsmouth Historic Zone Base Map.

[290] Joe A. Mobley, *Ship Ashore! The U. S. Lifesavers of Coastal North Carolina*, Raleigh, N. C.: Division of Archives and History, N. C. Department of Cultural Resources, 1994.

[291] Williamson, *Unsung Heroes of the Surf*, 79.

[292] *Ibid.*

[293] Sarah Olson, "Historic Resource Study, Portsmouth Village," Cape Lookout National Seashore, N. C., Denver, Col.: United States Department of the Interior, National Parks Service, March 1983, 89.

[294] Ben Salter, Interview with an unknown person, 10 January 1978.

[295] Salter, *Portsmouth Island: Short Stories and History*, 42.

[296] Mobley, *Ships Ashore! The U. S. Lifesavers of Coastal North Carolina*.

[297] Williamson, *Unsung Heroes of the Surf*, 80.

[298] Lucy Gilgo, Collection of Photographs of Portsmouth Island taken 1922, in possession of the author.

[299] *The Mailboat*, Spring 1992, vol. 3, No. 1, p. 6.

[300] *Ibid.*, 6.

[301] *Ibid.*

[302] *Ibid.*

[303] *Ibid.*

[304] Portsmouth Historic Zone Base Map.

[305] Salter, *Portsmouth Island: Short Stories and History*, 53.

[306] *The Mailboat*, Spring 1992, Vol. 3, No. 1, p. 6.

[307] *Ibid.*

[308] *Ibid.*

[309] Salter, *Portsmouth Island: Short Stories and History,* 53.

[310] Lionel Gilgo, Interview with Jim Godwin, Portsmouth, 17 July 1978.

[311] Calvin J. O'Neal, Alice K. Rondthaler, and Anita Fletcher, "The Story of Ocracoke," in *Hyde County History: A Hyde County Bicentennial Project* (Swan Quarter, N. C.: Hyde County Historical Society, 1976), 9.

[312] Lionel Gilgo, Interview with Jim Godwin, Portsmouth, 15 July 1978.

[313] Steven Roberts, Interview with William Mansfield, Morehead City, 23 June 1982.

[314] *Ibid.*

[315] White, *The Gilgoes of Portsmouth Island and Related Families*, 69.

[316] Federal Census of the United States, 1860, 1870, & 1880.

[317] Carteret County Marriage License, Beaufort, N. C.: Carteret County Court House, Register of Deeds Office.

[318] Eula Pearl Beauchamp, Interview with the author, New Bern, N. C.: 30 June 1997.

[319] Federal Census of the United States, 1850.

[320] Federal Census of the United States, 1860.

[321] Bettie Hartsell, Interview with the author, New Bern, N. C.: 29 June 1997.

[322] Federal Census of the United States, 1900.

[323] *In Memory of. . . Hyde County Cemeteries*, 1973, 316.

[324] *Ibid.*

[325] *Ibid.*

[326] *Ibid.*

[327] Elma Morgan Dixon, Interview with Nancy Godwin and Rebecca Harriett, Beaufort, N. C.: 18 August 1979.

[328] Louie Dixon, Interview with Don Davis, 10 January 1978.

[329] Nora Fulcher, Interview with William Mansfield, Oriental, N. C.: 30 June 1982.

[330] *Ibid.*

[331] Lionel Gilgo, Interview with Jim Godwin, Portsmouth, 15 July 1978.

[332] Sarah Roberts Styron, Interview with Nancy Godwin, Beaufort, N. C.: 31 December 1978.

[333] Cecil Gilgo and Leona Gilgo, Interview with Connie Mason, Davis, N. C.: 8 March 1985.

[334] Olson, "Historic Resource Study, Portsmouth Village," 70.

[335] *Ibid.*

[336] Burke, *The History of Portsmouth Island,* 39.

[337] *Ibid.*

[338] Lionel Gilgo, Interview with Jim Godwin, Portsmouth, 15 July 1978.

339 *Ibid.*

340 Lucy Gilgo, Interview with William Mansfield, Oriental, 31 July 1982.

341 Louie Dixon, Interview with Don Davis, et. al., 10 January 1978.

342 Steve Roberts, Interview with William Mansfield, Morehead City, 9 July 1982.

343 Williamson, *Unsung Heroes of the Surf*, 80.

344 Sarah Roberts Styron, Interview with Nancy Godwin, Beaufort, N. C.: 31 December 1978.

345 White, *The Gilgoes of Portsmouth Island and Related Families*, 25

346 *Ibid.*

347 Eula Pearl Beauchamp and Jo Ann Ernul Murphy, Addendum, Cedar Grove Cemetery (oldest part), New Bern, N. C.: privately printed, n.d.

348 Ellen Fulcher Cloud, "Civil War Census of Portsmouth Island, roll of White Male Citizens of Portsmouth, NC between the ages of 18 and 35 years," (http://familytreemaker.genealogy.com/users/c/l/o/Ellen -F-Cloud/FILE/0007page.html).

349 Mattie Daly Gilgo, Interview with Julian Gilgo, 1963 (Ellen Fulcher Cloud, *Portsmouth: The Way it Was* (Ocracoke, N. C.: Live Oak Publications, 1996), 167.

350 White, *The Gilgoes of Portsmouth Island and Related Families*, 25.

351 *Ibid.*

352 Carteret County Register of Deeds, Beaufort, NC: Book U, pp. 496-497 (4 August 1828).

353 Carteret County Register of Deeds, Beaufort, NC: Book Y, p. 134 (30 March 1837).

354 Carteret County Register of Deeds, Beaufort, N. C.: Book PP. p. 89 (15 June 1888).

355 Carteret County Register of Deeds, Book 142, p. 287 24

356 Nora Roberts Fulcher, Interview with the Author, Oriental, N. C.: 18 July 1997.

357 *Ibid.*

358 Carteret County Register of Deeds, Beaufort, N. C.: Book 142, p. 287, 24 July 1919.

359 White, *The Gilgoes of Portsmouth Island and Related Families*, 37.

360 Carteret County Register of Deeds, Deed Book SS, p. 501,

361 *Ibid.*

362 White, *The Gilgoes of Portsmouth Island and Related Familes*, 31.

363 Cloud, Federal Census for 1900.

364 White, *The Gilgoes of Portsmouth Island and Related Families*, 32.

[365] Nora Roberts Fulcher, Interview with the Author, Oriental, N. C.: 18 July 1997.

[366] Pearl Beauchamp (Interview at her home, New Bern, NC: 29 January 2010).

[367] Virginia Salter Laughinghouse, New Bern, N. C.: Unpublished paper on the life of John Wallace Salter, n.d.

[368] Dudley, *Carteret Waterfowl Heritage*, 65.

[369] *Ibid.*

[370] Pearl Williams Beauchamp, Interview with the author, New Bern, N. C.: 30 July 1996.

[371] *Ibid.*

[372] Dot Willis, Interview with the author, Morehead City, N. C.: 3 June 2010.

[373] Pearl Williams Beauchamp, Interview with the author, New Bern, N. C.: 30 July 1996.

[374] Dot Willis, Interview with the author, Morehead City, N. C.: 3 June 2010.

[375] Nora Fulcher Roberts, Interview with William Mansfield, Oriental, N. C.: 30 June 1982.

[376] *Ibid.*

[377] Pearl Williams Beauchamp, Interview with the author, New Bern, N. C.: 30 July 1996.

[378] Dot Willis, Interview with the author, Morehead City, N. C.: 3 June 2010.

[379] Federal Census of the United States, 1850-1880.

[380] Carteret County Marriage Bonds, Beaufort, N. C.

[381] Federal Census of the United States, Carteret County, N. C., 1850.

[382] Carteret County Marriage Bonds, Beaufort, North Carolina.

[383] Federal Census of the United States, Carteret County, N. C.: 1910.

[384] Ben Salter, *Portsmouth Island: Short Stories and History* (Privately Published, 1972), 5.

[385] White, *The Gilgoes of Portsmouth Island and Related Families*, 51.

[386] *Ibid.*

[387] Eula Pearl Beauchamp, Interview with the author, New Bern, N. C.: 3 August 1996.

[388] John D. Mayo's Family Bible Records, in possession of Jean Webber.

[389] *Ibid.*

[390] Salter, *Portsmouth Island: Short Stories and History,* 22.

[391] *Ibid.*

[392] *Ibid.*

[393] Federal Census of the United States, Carteret County, N. C.: 1850-1880.

[394] *Ibid.*, 1860.

[395] Carteret County Marriage Bonds, Beaufort, N. C.

[396] Federal Census of the United States, Carteret County, North Carolina, 1870.

[397] Atlantic Community Cemetery, Atlantic, N. C.

[398] Lionel Gilgo and Emma Gilgo, Interview with William Mansfield, Atlantic, N. C.: 16 June 1982.

[399] Dot Salter Willis and Ben B. Salter, *Portsmouth Island: Short Stories & History* (Privately published, 2004), 14.

[400] Federal Census, 1910.

[401] Eula Pearl Williams Beauchamp, Interview with author, New Bern, N. C.: 3 August 1996.

[402] *Ibid.*

[403] http://www.nccoastwatch.org/index.cfm?fuseaction=story&pubid=138&storyid=203.

[404] Dudley, *Carteret Waterfowl Heritage*, 37.

[405] *Ibid.*

[406] *Ibid.*, 38.

[407] *Ibid.*

BIBLIOGRAPHY

Abbott, Jeremiah. Deed to John Valentine Bragg. Beaufort, N. C. Carteret County Register of Deeds, Book CC, p. 181, 17 September 1866.

Abbott, Jeremiah. Deed to William T. Etheridge. Beaufort, N. C. Carteret County Register of Deeds, Book CC, p. 26, 1866.

Allegood, Jerry. "Researchers dive into history in Ocracoke Inlet." *The News and Observer* (13 May, 1995).

Babb, Marian Gray. Interview with Nancy Godwin. 26 July 1978.

Babb, Marian Gray and Clara Salter Gaskins. Interview with Nancy Godwin. 9 August 1979.

Barbour, Ruth. "Portsmouth Won't Be the Same." *Carteret County News-Times*, 18 January 1971.

Beauchamp, Eula Pearl Williams. Interview with James E. White, III. New Bern, N. C.: 30 June 1997.

Beauchamp, Eula Pearl Williams, and Jo Ann Murphy. *Addendum, Cedar Grove Cemetery (Oldest Part)* (New Bern, N. C.: privately published, n.d.).

Beauchamp, Eula Pearl Williams, and Jo Ann Murphy. *1860 Census of Craven County, North Carolina* (New Bern, N. C.: privately published, n. d.).

Beauchamp, Eula Pearl Williams, Jo Ann Murphy, and Jerline (Jere) S. Wetherington. *Craven County, North Carolina Cemeteries Volume 1, City of New Bern* (New Bern, N. C.: The Eastern North Carolina Genealogical Society, n.d.).

Bedwell, Dorothy Byrum. *Portsmouth: Island with a Soul.* (New Bern, N. C.: IES Publications, 1984).

Brown, Sylvester, deed to Earles Ireland. Beaufort, N. C.: Carteret County Register of Deeds, Book WW, p. 550, 7 November 1901.

Burke, Kenneth E., Jr. *The History of Portsmouth,* North Carolina From the Founding in 1753 to its Evacuation in the Face of Federal Forces in 1861. (Washington, D. C.: Insta-Print, Inc., 1976).

Civil War Soldiers and Sailors System,http://www.civilwar.nps.gov/cwss/Personz-Detail.cfm Charles B. Keeler

Cloud, Ellen Fulcher. "Civil War Census of Portsmouth Island, roll of white Male citizens of Portsmouth, N. C. between the ages of 18 and 35 years." (http://familytreemaker.genealogy.com/users/c/l/o.Ellen-F-Cloud/FILE/0007page.html).

Cloud, Ellen Fulcher. *The Federal Census of Portsmouth Island, N. C.* (Ocracoke, N. C.: Live Oak Publications, n.d.).

Cloud, Ellen Fulcher. Interview with James E. White, III. July 2009.

Cloud, Ellen Fulcher. *Portsmouth: The Way it Was* (Ocracoke, N. C.: Live Oak Publications, 1996).

Dixon, Elijah. Deed to Mattie Gilgo. Beaufort, N. C.: Carteret County, Register of Deeds, Book 9, p. 410, 15 July 1910.

Dixon, Elma Morgan. Interview with Nancy Godwin and Rebecca Harriett. Beaufort, N. C.: 18 August 1979.

Dixon, Louie. Interview with Don Davis, et. al. 10 January 1978.

Dixon, Nina Mann. Interview with James E. White, III. Oriental, N. C.: Winter/Spring, 1976.

Dixon, Nina Mann. Interview with James E. White, III. Oriental, N. C.: 2 February 1977.

Dudley, Jack. *Carteret Waterfowl Heritage*. (Morehead City, N. C.: Decoy Magazine, 1993).

Dudley, Dr. Samuel. New Bern, N. C.: Cedar Grove Cemetery, Gravestone.

Federal Census of the United States, 1860. Wallingford, New Haven, Connecticut, Roll M653_84, p. 401.

Fulcher, Nora. Interview with William Mansfield. Oriental, N. C.: 30 June 1982.

Fulcher, Nora. Interview with James E. White, III. Oriental, N. C. 18 July 1997.

Gilgo, Cecil, and Iona Gilgo. Interview with Connie Mason. Davis, N. C.: 8 March 1985.

Gilgo, Lionel. Interview with Jim Godwin. Portsmouth, N. C.: 15 July 1978.

Gilgo, Lionel. Interview with Cat Troutman. Portsmouth, N. C.: 24 September 1981.

Gilgo, Lionel, and Emma Gilgo. Interview with William Mansfield. Atlantic, N. C.: 7 July 1982.

Gilgo, Lucy Beacham. Interview with James E. White, III. Oriental, N. C.: 1980.

Gilgo, Mattie Daly. Interview with Julian Gilgo, 1963 in Ellen Fulcher Cloud, *Portsmouth: The Way It Was* (Ocracoke, N. C.: Live Oak Publication, 1996).

Goodwin, Henry. Deed to Alfred Dixon. Beaufort, N. C.: Carteret County Register of Deeds, book 4, p. 59, 29 September 1904.

Hall, Archibald. Deed to Wallis Styron. Beaufort, N. C.: Carteret County Register of Deeds, book U, p. 415, 8 August 1828.

Hardy, Daniel. Deed to William W. Dixon. Beaufort, N. C.: Carteret County Register of Deeds, Book U, pp. 496-497, 4 August 1828.

Hartsell, Bettie. Interview with James E. White, III. New Bern, N. C.: 29 June 1997.

Heady, David. Deed to Denard Roberts. Beaufort, N. C.: Carteret County Register of Deeds, book Y, p. 134, 20 April, 1840.

Heady, Daniel. Deed to David Wallace. Beaufort, N. C.: Carteret County Register of Deeds, book Y, p. 134, 30 March 1837.

"Historic Property Leasing Program." Cape Lookout National Seashore Request for Proposals, Portsmouth Village, 1992.

Holland, Ross F., Jr. "A Survey History of Cape Lookout National Seashore." (Washington, D. C.: Department of the Interior, National Parks Service, Division of History, Office of Archaeology and History Preservation, 1968).

Ireland, Earles. Beaufort, N. C.: Carteret County Register of Deeds, book SS, p. 501, 1841.

Keeler, Annie McCotter. New Bern, N. C.: Craven County Register of Deeds, Death Certificates, #22883, 7 September 1920.

Keeler, Charles. Marriage to Martha A. McCotter. New Bern, N. C.: Craven County Register of Deeds, Marriage Register, Volume 1, p. 80, 29 January 1865.

Keeler, Charles. Deed to F. G. Terrell. Beaufort, N. C.: Carteret County Register of Deeds, book UU, p. 387, 20 August 1898.

Keeler, Charles. Deed to James R. Willis. Beaufort, N. C.: Carteret County Register of Deeds, book ZZ, pp. 34-35, 23 November 1898.

Keeler, Martha. Deed to E. G. Dixon. Beaufort, N. C.: Carteret County Register of Deeds, book 6, p. 297, 11 December 1907.

Keeler Tombstones. New Bern, N. C.: Cedar Grove Cemetery.

Laughinghouse, Virginia Salter. New Bern, N. C.: Unpublished paper on the life of John Wallace Salter, n.d. *The Mailboat,* Harkers Island, N. C.: Spring, 1992.

Mallison, Fred M. *The Civil War on the Outer Banks: A History of the Late Rebellion Along the Coast of North Carolina From Carteret to Currituck.* (Jefferson, N. C.: McFarland & Company, Inc., Publishers, 1998.).

Mason, Connie. "Timeline: Portsmouth and Nearby Islands." *The Mailboat* (Harkers Island, N. C.: Spring, 1992).

Mayo, John D. Deed to Sylvester H. Gray. Beaufort, N. C.: Carteret County Register of Deeds, book CC, p. 102, 3 April 1867.

Mobley, Joe A. *Ship Ashore! The U. S. Lifesavers of Coastal North Carolina* (Raleigh, N. C.: Division of Archives and History, North Carolina Department of Cultural Resources, 1994).

Nelson, Frances. Deed to Archibald Hall. Beaufort, N. C.: Carteret County Register of Deeds, book T, pp 128-129, 13 January 1824.

New Bern Daily Journal. 20 January 1885.

New Bern Daily Times. 11 October 1871.

New Bern Weekly Journal. 21 July 1899.

New Bern Weekly Journal. 17 October 1905.

"Notes from Shell Castle." Harkers Island, N. C.: *The Mail Boat*: Spring, 1992.

O'Neal, Calvin J., Alice K. Rondthalen and Anita Fletcher. "The Story of Ocracoke" in *Hyde County: A Hyde County Bicentennial Project* (Swan Quarter, N. C.: Hyde County Historical Society, 1976).

Olson, Sarah. "Historic Resource Study, Portsmouth Village, Cape Lookout National Seashore, N. C. Denver, Co.: United States Department of Interior, National Park Service, March, 1982.

"Portsmouth Historic Zone Map" Washington, D.C.: United States Department of Interior, National Park Service, Cape Lookout National Seashore, n.d.

Rew, Southy. Deed to Richard Casey. Carteret County Register of Deeds, Beaufort, N. C.: Book O, p. 54, 21 October 1797.

Roberts, Joe. Deed to Jim Roberts. Beaufort, N. C.: Carteret County Register of Deeds, book PP, p. 89, 15 June 1888.

Roberts, Joe. Deed to Tom Gilgo. Beaufort, N. C.: Carteret County Register of Deeds, book 142, p. 287, 24 July 1919.

Roberts, Mary B. Deed to Alexander Robinson. Beaufort, N. C.: Carteret County Register of Deeds, book MM, p. 390, 9 November 1884.

Roberts, Steve. Interview with William Mansfield. Morehead City, N. C.: 9 July 1982.

Roberts, Steve. Interview with William Mansfield. Morehead City, N. C.: 30 July 1982.

Roberts, Steve, and Clayton Willis. Interview with William Mansfield. Atlantic, N. C.: 3 August 1982.

Roberts, Steve. Interview with William Mansfield. Portsmouth, N. C.: 3 September 1982.

Salsi, Lynn, and Frances Eubanks. *The Crystal Coast.* (Charleston, S. C.: Arcadia Publishing, 2000).

Salter, Ben. Atlantic, N. C.: Interview. 10 January 1978.

Salter, Ben B. *Portsmouth Island: Short Stories and History* (Privately Published, 1972).

Salter, Dot. Interview with James E. White, III. Morehead City, N. C.: 3 August 1996.

Salter, Dot. Interview with Jim Godwin. Portsmouth, N. C.: 15 July 1978.

Salter, Dot, and Ben B. Salter. *Portsmouth Island: Short Stories & History* (Privately Published, 2004).

Sparrow, Thomas. Deed to Charles Keeler. Beaufort, N. C.: Carteret County Register of Deeds, book LL, p. 53, 1883.

Styron, Sarah Roberts. Interview with Nancy Godwin. Beaufort, N. C.: 31 December 1978.

Styron, Wallis. Deed to Jeremiah Abbott. Beaufort, N. C.: Carteret County Register of Deeds, book CC, p. 180, 10 July 1857.

Tolson, Sam. Marriage License. New Bern, N. C.: Craven County Register of Deeds, Marriage License, book 3, p. 380, 19 February 1870.

Tolson, Sam. Death Certificate. Beaufort, N. C.: Carteret County Register of Deeds, Death Certificates, Vol 12, p.1 87, 30 November 1929.

Wallace, David. Deed to David Heady. Beaufort, N. C.: Carteret County Register of Deeds, book U, pp. 9-10, 18 April 1826.

Wallace, David. Beaufort, N. C.: Carteret County Register of Deeds, book W, p. 379, 22 April 1835.

White, James E., III. *The Gilgoes of Portsmouth Island and Related Families* (New Bern, N. C.: The Eastern North Carolina Genealogical Society, 1979).

White, Sherry. "When life was young in a village called Portsmouth." Morehead City, N. C.: *The News-Times*, 9 June 1995.

Williamson, Sonny. *Unsung Heroes of the Surf: the Life Saving Service of Carteret County* (Marshallburg, N. C.: Grandma Publications, 1992).

Willis, Milan. Deed to Harry Dixon. Beaufort, N. C.: Carteret County Register of Deeds, book 61, p. 179, 18 June 1930.

INDEX

The numbers given beside the items refer to the individual articles and not to the pages.

Abbott, Elizabeth Brent	29	Bell, Joseph	vii
Abbott, Jeremiah	29	Ben Salter's Camp	86
Abbott, Joe	45, 51, 56	Blount, John Gray	3, 4
Abbott, Mary Bateman	29	Bookhart, Jack	20
Abbott, Maude Owen	29	Booth, John Wilkes	24
Abbott, Thomas H.	29	Bragg, Annie	28, 29
Academy	37, 67, 77, 78	Bragg, Bulah	29, 88
Academy Green	78	Bragg, Caroline "Lina"	29, 73
Academy Pond	78	Bragg, Jane A. Gaskill	23, 73
Allen, Virginia	71	Bragg, John V.	23, 29, 73, 88
Anaconda	2	Bragg, Joseph	29
Armtex Co.	31	Bragg, Tom	7, 22, 23, 24, 25, 28, 29, 46, 47, 88
Artisan Well	2		
Atlas	2		
Austin, Harem	21	Brooks, George	74
Austin, Junius	21	Brown, Sylvester	14
Austin, Rudy	viii, 5, 32	Burgess, Ed	iii, v
Austin, Capt. William	84	Burgess, Rene	iii, v
Babb, Edna Earl	54	Burgess, Theresa	10
Babb, George Rodnal	34	Burns, Capt. Ottway	49
Babb, Harry	8, 12, 20, 41, 44, 54	Byrum, Augusta Holly	12
		Byrum, Dorothy	12, 20
Babb, Henry, Jr.	12	Campbell, John	vii
Babb, Hugh Linwood	34	Carrington, Charles D.	57
Babb, Jesse	8, 12, 46, 54, 55	Carrington, Jeanne B.	7
		Casey, Richard	2
Babb, Jesse Lee	54	Casey's Island	1, 2, 3, 43
Babb, Lillian M.	48, 54	Cheatham, Don	56
Babb, Joseph	12	Cisterns	14, 44
Babb, Marian Gray	viii, 48, 54	Civil War	4, 14, 21, 24, 27, 29, 33, 56, 62, 80, 100
Babb, Mary Dixon	12		
Babb, Sarah J.	98		
Babb, Virginia S.	98		
Ballast Stone Hill	38, 39	Clark, Elisha C.	30
Bateman, Mary	29	Clark, William C.	30
Battle Boys Camp	99	Cloud, Ellen Marie Fulcher	iii
Beacham, Lucy	20	Coast Guard Station	(See Life Saving Station)
Beacon Island	4		
Beauchamp, Eula Pearl	9, 24, 74, 87, 88, 92, 93	Cockburn, George	2
		Coe, Jeffrey	10
Bedwell, Dorothy Byrum	12	Community Cemetery	34

Contanoh, Michael	vii	Dixon, Lida (Lydia)	34, 38, 57
Croquet	36	Dixon, Lillian	54
Dairy	47	Dixon, Louise	46
Daly, Blanche Gilgo	34	Dixon, Mandy Jane	10
Daly, Claudia Williams	27, 34	Dixon, Martha	34
Davis, Mary J.	30	Dixon, Mary	12
Daly, William	34, 44	Dixon, Mary E.	34
Daly, William T.	27, 34, 38	Dixon, Mary F.	30
Davis, Catherine	92	Dixon, Mary Helen	34
Day, Almira Dudley	50	Dixon, Mary Sneeden	33
Dennis, A. W.	25, 29	Dixon, Mildred	57
Dennis, Alphius E.	97	Dixon, Nora	43, 48
Dick	48	Dixon, Patsy	46, 57
Dipping Vat	77	Dixon, Russell	30
Dixon-Babb House	44	Dixon, Sarah James	12, 20, 71, 79, 81, 94
Dixon, Abner	30		
Dixon, Adelaide	30	Dixon, Solomon	43
Dixon, Alfred	13, 14, 34	Dixon, Sylvanius	30
Dixon, Ann	31	Dixon, Wilford D.	30, 34
Dixon, Arthur Edward	48	Dixon, William	45
Dixon, Benjamin R.	23, 30	Dixon, William C., Sr.	30, 34
Dixon, Carl	13, 14, 22, 44	Dixon, William C., Jr.	30, 100
Dixon, Carolet	30	Dixon, William G.	12, 14, 94
Dixon, Corbet	30	Dixon, William W.	81
Dixon, Ed	7, 8, 22, 46, 47, 48, 52, 54	Doctor's Creek	2, 46, 49, 52, 62
Dixon, Edith	30	Dorcas	51
Dixon, E. G.	33	Dorothy	51
Dixon, Elijah	38	Duane, Arthur	105
Dixon, Elma Morgan	viii, 8, 32, 45	Dudley, Almira	49, 50
Dixon, Emeline Salter	12	Dudley, Augustus	49
Dixon, Ernestine	30	Dudley, Elizabeth	49
Dixon, Estelle	30	Dudley, Jack	25
Dixon, Eugene	34	Dudley, John Potts	49
Dixon, George	31, 34, 46	Dudley, John Wesley	49
Dixon, George C.	2, 34, 43, 44, 57	Dudley, Mary Catherine	49
Dixon, George S.	12, 14, 44, 81, 100	Dudley, Dr. Samuel	19, 42, 45, 49, 50, 51, 62
Dixon, Georgia M.	23	Dudley, Samuel, Jr.	49, 50
Dixon, Harry Needam	7, 34, 54, 57	Dudley, Susan D.	45, 49, 50
Dixon, Helen A.	70	Dudley, Susan Saulsbury	49, 50
Dixon, Joe	7, 9, 44, 61, 67, 74, 76	Emery, Lydia Ann	93
		Emery, Mary "Martha"	91

English, Rebecca	69		Gaskill, Jane Ann	75
Etheridge, Emma	29		Gaskill, John	24
Etheridge, Julia Gilgo	29		Gaskill, John W.	15, 16, 75
Etheridge, Mary L.	29		Gaskill, Joseph Earls	75, 81
Etheridge, Thomas	29		Gaskill, Mary E.	75, 81
Etheridge, William T.	29		Gaskill, Matilda	75
Excelsior Oil and Guano Company	2		Gaskill, Penelope	24
			Gaskill, Stephen A.	75
Farmer, Sidney	57		Gaskill, Steve	75
Fish Factory	43		Gaskill, Susan J.	23
Forts	4		Gaskill, Thomas S.	23
Fort Morgan	4		Gaskill, Winnie	24, 30, 75
Fort Ocracoke	4		Gaskins, Elizabeth Daly	34
Freemasons	7, 34, 46, 56, 57, 76, 84		Gaskins, Sarah Jane	71
			George II	vii
Fulcher, Alice	96		Gilgo, Angeline "Angie"	80
Fulcher, Alladin	101		Gilgo, Anson	80
Fulcher, Claughton	101		Gilgo, Bill	67, 80, 94
Fulcher, Edward	58, 101		Gilgo, Blanche	81
Fulcher, Elva Christian Midgett	96, 101		Gilgo, Carolna "Lina" Bragg	29
			Gilgo, Cecil	35, 36, 93
Fulcher, Fannie	101		Gilgo, Elizabeth	34, 84
Fulcher, Harris	89, 101		Gilgo, Elmo	81
Fulcher, Jerome	101		Gilgo, Emeline Robinson	38, 68, 83
Fulcher, Job	101		Gilgo, Emma	38, 51, 59
Fulcher, John	101		Gilgo, George Wallis	29, 61, 67, 68, 72, 73, 80
Fulcher, Levin	101			
Fulcher, Lina	89		Gilgo, Goldie	83
Fulcher, Lucile	89		Gilgo, James Monroe	86, 94
Fulcher, Manson	86, 96, 101		Gilgo, James Warren	67, 80, 82, 83, 88
Fulcher, Nora Roberts	88			
Fulcher, Sabra Elizabeth	89		Gilgo, Julia	29
Fulcher, William	101		Gilgo, Lemmie	71, 75, 81, 82
Garrish, Simon	22, 43, 46, 47, 48, 61		Gilgo, Leona	36
			Gilgo, Lionel	13, 51, 59
Gaskill, Betsy	81		Gilgo, Lucy Beacham	iv, 20
Gaskill, Elijah	16, 75		Gilgo, Lydia	80
Gaskill, Elijah T.	75		Gilgo, Mahettable Wallace	80
Gaskill, Elizabeth L.	15, 16		Gilgo, Major	80
Gaskill, Frank	15, 16, 44, 75		Gilgo, Mary Roseland	71
			Gilgo, Mattie	38, 39, 44, 45, 51
Gaskill, Gladys	87			
Gaskill, James	80		Gilgo, Rita Johnson	34

Gilgo, Ronald Linwood	71	Herring, Louise Brown	38
Gilgo, Ruby	83	Hill, Bobby	87
Gilgo, Sarah	71, 80	Hill, John	104
Gilgo, Sarah James	12, 20, 79	Hill, Peter	104
Gilgo, Sophronia	14, 82, 83	Hilzey, Capt. William	63
Gilgo, Susan Jane	80, 81	Howard, George	57
Gilgo, Theressa	80	Ireland, Daniel	14
Gilgo, Vera	57, 68, 72, 80	Ireland, David	14, 56
		Ireland, Earles	7, 14, 19, 21, 51, 56, 78, 82, 83
Gilgo, Virginia	71		
Gilgo, William	38, 68, 73, 80, 81		
		Ireland, Eula	99
Gilgo, William Tom	61, 72, 80, 94	Ireland, Love	78
		Ireland, Mary	14
Gilgo, William Tom, Sr.	12, 20, 57, 71, 72, 77, 79, 80, 81, 82, 83, 94	Ireland, Matilda	14
		Ireland, Mattie	51
		Jackson, Mary Eliza	70
		S. S. Jamestown	93
Gilgo, William Tom, Jr.	20, 21, 41, 55, 61, 67, 81	John I Snow	38
		Junior Order of Union of American Machinists and Mechanics	16
Gilgo, Willis Monroe	34, 38, 80	Keeler, Annie	6, 25, 33
Gilgo Cemetery	84	Keeler, Charlie	6, 25, 32, 33, 38
Gilgo Creek	34, 40		
Goins, Jim	105	Keeler, Ed	25, 26, 32, 33
Gooding, Rebecca Ann	81	Keeler, Martha	33, 38
Goodwin, Henry	14, 57	Keeler, William	32, 33
Goodwin, Lena	57	Keeler Cemetery	32
Goodwin, Wilbert	46	Kemp, Arthur	105
Grace, John B.	11	Kemp, Atwater	60
Grace, John K.	10, 11	Kersey, John	vi
Grace, Theresa Burgess	10, 11	"Kitty Cabin"	53
Grace, William	11	Lawrence, Hannah	32
Gray, Sylvester H.	25	Leech, Joseph	vii
Green, Capt. Thomas W.	63	Life Saving Station	10, 20, 22, 24, 25, 26, 38, 44, 46, 54, 56, 58, 59, 61, 62, 73, 93
Griffin, George A.	30		
Grist Mill	14, 19		
Guthrie & Jones Drug Store	17		
Hall, Archibald	38		
Haulover	1, 2		
Heady, Daniel	81	Lightering	4
Heady, David	31	Lighthouse	3, 6
Herring, Charles Henry	38	Lincoln, Abraham	24

Lola Cemetery	69	Mayo, Susan	97
The Lorena Dee	76	Mayo, Warren L.	97
Lovat, Richard	vi	Mayo, William	97
Lynn, Chester	iv	McCotter, Charlie	25
Maffitt, David	2	McCotter, John T.	33
Mail boat	13	McCotter, Martha A.	33
Mann, Asa	14	McCotter, Narcissa E. Paul	25, 33
Mann, Matilda Ireland	14	McCotter, Susan Dena	25, 33
Mann, Nina	14, 80	Meekins, Mozell	69
Manson, Sarah	75	Menhaden Fish Factory	2
Marine Hospital	44, 49, 51, 59, 61, 62	Midgette, Annie	101
		Midgette, Crissie	101
Mason, Alvin	105	Morris Marina	viii, 65
Mason, Amelia	105	Mott, Jordan L.	105
Mason, Augustus D.	61	Nelson, Frances J. W.	33
Mason, Dennis	57, 61	Newton, Archibald	91
Mason, Francis	90	Newton, Bennett	91
Mason, Mamie	90	Newton, Charles	91
Mason, Sarah	103	Newton, Cora	91
Mason, Susan	101	Newton, James S.	91
Mason, W. R.	90	Newton, Jessie	91
Mayo, Barbara	97	Newton, Jessie T.	61
Mayo, Benjamin F.	97	Newton, Joshua	91
Mayo, Comfort	97	Newton, Martha	91
Mayo, Edward	97	Newton, Mary C.	91
Mayo, Elizaer	97	Newton, Vertie	91
Mayo, George	97	Newton, William	91
Mayo, Hannah	97	Newton, William B.	91
Mayo, James	97	North West Point Lighthouse	6, 33
Mayo, James	97	Ocracoke Inlet	4
Mayo, John	78, 97	Ocracoke Island	5, 9
Mayo, John D.	25, 78, 97, 97	Oglesby, John W.	94
		Oglesby, Lucy	94
Mayo, Marcus	78, 97	O'Neal, Joe	51
Mayo, Margaret	78	O'Neal, Stanley	69
Mayo, Margaretta	97	Outhouse	8
Mayo, Mayo	97	Parsons, Alice	70
Mayo, Milard	98	Parsons, Amelia	70
Mayo, Milton	97	Parsons, Elizabeth	18
Mayo, Nancy	23	Parsons, Frederic	70
Mayo, Rebecca	97	Parsons, George	57, 70
Mayo, Sarah	97	Parsons, George Lewis	70
Mayo, Sidney W.	97	Parsons, Jim	67, 70

Parsons, Joseph O.	70	Roberts, Holland	75
Parsons, Mary H.	34	Roberts, James W.	67, 81
Parsons, Mary Susan	70	Roberts, Jenny	56
Parsons, Samuel	70	Roberts, Joe	60, 81, 82
Paul, Narcissa E.	25, 33	Roberts, John	14
Pete	48	Roberts, John B.	34
Pigott, Elizabeth	21, 48	Roberts, Jonsey	56
Pigott, Georgia	51	Roberts, Martha "Patsey"	88, 95
Pigott, Harriett	51	Roberts, Mary B.	31
Pigott, Henry	vi, viii, 8, 9, 21, 22, 28, 32, 45, 46, 47, 48, 51, 55	Roberts, Mary E.	34
		Roberts, Matilda	14
		Roberts, Nora	88, 89, 101
		Roberts, Norwood	88, 89
Pigott, Isaac	51	Roberts, Rebecca	81
Pigott, Leah	19, 21, 32, 51	Roberts, Sabra	86, 88, 89
		Roberts, Sarah	10
Pigott, Lizzie	21, 28, 48, 51	Roberts, Steve	81
		Roberts, Verona	81
Pigott, Nettie	51	Roberts, Washington	7, 14, 51, 56, 61
Pigott, Rachel	21, 23, 51		
Pigott, Rose	19, 21, 32, 51	Roberts, William	34
		Robertson, Jake	57
Pigott, Sarah	51	Robertson, Mildred	57
Pilentary Club House	86	Robinson, Alexander	23, 31
Pilot	12	Robinson, Annie	69, 92
Portsmouth Methodist Church	45, 51, 62, 68	Robinson, Billy	92
		Robinson, Cora	86, 92
Post Office	3, 9, 12	Robinson, Emeline	38, 68, 72, 73, 80, 81, 83
Potter, T. T.	31		
Potts, Dr. John W.	49, 62		
Primitive Baptist Church	67, 73, 78, 79	Robinson, James	23, 80
		Robinson, Jane Ann	23
Rew, Beverly	2	Robinson, Joseph W.	57
Rew, Southy	2	Robinson, Roy	59, 61
Roberson, Emeline	92	Robinson, Sidney	92
Roberts, Ada	81	Robinson, Sparrow	92
Roberts, Albert R.	90	Robinson, William	92
Roberts, Alec	81	Rogers, Theodore	105
Roberts, Denard	31, 81, 89	Roosevelt, Franklin D.	105
Roberts, Eason Thomas	90	Rose, Pennsylvania	104
Roberts, Elsa	10, 34	Rose, Sidney	104
Roberts, George	81	Ross Salter Camp	87
Roberts, Hannah	81	Rumley, John	9, 18

Ruth, Babe	87	School House	37, 77, 78, 79
Salter, Ada	99		
Salter, Annie	7, 8, 9	Shaler, Nathaniel	2
Salter, Benjamin	93	Sheep Island	36, 40, 86, 53
Salter, Billy	100		
Salter, Charlie	99	Shell Castle	3, 4, 5, 18, 98
Salter, Christopher	58, 69, 83, 87, 88, 89, 103	Shell Castle Island	3, 4, 5
		Singleton, _____	2
Salter, Dave	7, 88	Smith, Mariah	24
Salter, Doris Evelyn	iv, 93	Smith, Sarah Ann	104
Salter, Dorothy M.	9	Sneeden, Mary	33
Salter, Edward Roscoe	99	Southwest Point Lighthouse	25, 33
Salter, Ellen Faye	99	Sparrow, Sidney	38
Salter, Emeline	12, 14, 100	Spencer, Edward D.	71
Salter, Ethel Marie	93	Spencer, Louisa	71, 82
Salter, Geraldine Farrar	93	Sparrow, Thomas G.	38
Salter, George T.	83	Spofford, Richard S.	57
Salter, Hulda E.	69	St. John's Parish	45
Salter, Ina	105	St. Lawrence	2
Salter, James T.	61	Stewart, Maria	23
Salter, John Wallace	7, 69, 87, 88, 93	Stewart, Oliver	23
		Store	9
Salter, Margaret Carolyn	93	Stowe, Berry	25
Salter, Mary	69, 81	Straight Road	35, 40, 43
Salter, Mary Elizabeth	58, 93, 95	Styron, A. J.	32
Salter, Mary "Polly"	100	Styron, Alex	12
Salter, Matilda Styron	58, 83, 93	Styron, Ambrose J.	35, 46
Salter, Polly	83, 100	Styron, Annie Bragg	29
Salter, Rebecca Lauren	99	Styron, Benj. G.	32
Salter, Ross	87	Styron, Charles H.	95
Salter, Sabra	89, 99	Styron, David	95
Salter, Sophronia	88	Styron, Ed	53, 102
Salter, Thelma Styron	93	Styron, Elsie	28
Salter, Theodore	7, 8, 9, 46, 60, 67, 74, 76, 88	Styron, Eugene	32
		Styron, George Washington	95
		Styron, Gracie	96
Salter, Tom	99	Styron, James	34, 70
Salter, William	83	Styron, J. D.	32
Salter, William Benjamin	93	Styron, Jennie	56
Salter, William W.	100	Styron, Jodie	7, 22, 24, 25, 28, 29, 46, 47, 56
Salter, Zachariah	67, 69		
Salter Gun Club	87		

Styron, John A.	103		Wallace, John	3, 4, 5, 18, 86, 98
Styron, John B.	95, 96			
Styron, Kate	53, 102		Wallace, Mahettable	80
Styron, Louisa	95		Wallace, Rebecca	86, 98
Styron, Lovie	80		Wallace, Sidney	18
Styron, Malinda	70		Wallace Channel	5, 65
Styron, Mary	70, 95		War of 1812	2, 4
Styron, Matilda	69, 83, 88, 89, 103		Warren Gilgo Creek	67
			Washington Greys	29
Styron, May	70		"Washington Row"	29
Styron, Sarah	10		Water Box	55
Styron, Sidney Jane	87, 93		Water Cistern	44
Styron, Stephen	95, 96		Webb, Will	2
Styron, Thelma	93		West Indies	29
Styron, Thomas W.	45		Whitehurst, David W.	18, 75
Styron, Walker	10, 22		Whitehurst, Lydia A.	75
Styron, Wallis	38, 45		Whitehurst, Melvira	18
Styron, William R.	93		Whitehurst, Richard	18
Styron, Zachariah	70, 88, 95		Whitehurst, Richard, Jr.	18
Summer Kitchen	22, 61		Whitehurst, Robert H.	18
Taylor, James	4		Whitehurst, Samuel	18
Terrell, Ferdinand G.	25, 26, 57, 61, 81		Whitehurst, Wallis	18, 45
			Williams, Bettie	34
Tice, William	57		Williams, Billy	36
Tin Building	17		Williams, Caroline	34
Tolson, Christopher	24		Williams, Claudia	27, 38, 44
Tolson, John	vii, 45		Williams, Esther	27, 43
Tolson, Mariah Smith	24		Williams, John	vii, 43, 44
Tolson, Penelope Gaskill	24		Williams, Patsy	43
Tolson, Sam	24, 32		Williams, William O.	34
Tom Salter Camp	86		Willis, Charles	57
U. S. Coast Guard (See Life Saving Station)			Willis, Clayton	58, 103
			Willis, Dave	57, 68
The Virginia Dare	57, 68		Willis, Dot Salter	88
The Vera Crus	26		Willis, Emeline Roberson	92
Wahab, Stanley	10		Willis, Emma	57
Walker, Jno.	33		Willis, George	103
Walker, Taylor	14		Willis, George R.	58, 95, 103
Wallace, Charlie	2, 10, 66		Willis, James	92
Wallace, David	1, 2, 14, 81		Willis, James R.	25
Wallace, David H.	18		Willis, Lena	57
Wallace, Elizabeth	66		Willis, Lida Mae	68
Wallace, James	14		Willis, Mahaley	57

Willis, Mary Ella	58, 95, 103
Willis, Milan	57, 67, 68, 72, 73
Willis, Missouri	57
Willis, Myron	68, 72
Willis, M. H.	72
Willis, R. T.	81
Willis, Rebekeah	92
Willis, Ronald G.	34
Willis, Sidney F.	57
Willis, Vera Gilgo	72
Willis, Will	25
Witterage and Wymore	4
Woolard, Stanley	40
World War I	71, 82
York, Harris W.	57
York, M. Franklin	57

PORTSMOUTH ISLAND: A Walk in the Past

Order Form

Web Orders: www.JamesEdwardWhite.com

Email Orders: info@JamesEdwardWhite.com

Postal Orders: James White, 405 W. Wilson Ck. Dr.
Trent Woods, N. C. 28562
Telephone 252-633-2586

____ **Copies of Portsmouth Island: A Walk into the Past @ 21.95** = _____

Sales Tax 7.75 % = _____
(Only for sales shipped to N. C. addresses)

Shipping & Handling @ 2.50 = _____

Total = _____

Name: _____

Address: _____

City: _____ **State** _____ **Zip** _____

Email Address _____

Payment: Check   Money Order